Taming the Monkey Mind

Mastering Your Thoughts for Inner Peace and Personal Transformation

A Self-Help Book for the Youngsters

To Inculcate Mindfulness, a Self-Compassionate Mindset, Worldly Wisdom, and Guidance from Shrimad Bhagavad Gita to Lead a Purposeful Life

Author: Madhu Sharma

TAMING THE MONKEY MIND

Copyright © Madhu Sharma, 2023

All rights reserved. No portion of this book may be reproduced in any form without permission from the publisher. For permission contact:

Publisher: Madhu Sharma

madhusharma2451@gmail

DEDICATION

Dedicated to my granddaughter Ishanvi and all my students whose experiences, dilemmas, and delusions inspired me to do some soul searching, to research and look for solutions to enable them to rise like phoenixes from the ashes of their turbulent minds to find their "eureka moment" and niche.

CONTENTS

Acknowledgments

Introduction

Part One- Taming the Monkey Mind: Mastering Your Thoughts for Inner Peace and Personal Transformation

1. Taming the Monkey Mind - 1

2. Create Conditions for Creativity -3

3. Let Us Learn to Live Amicably with Our Furry Friends- 6

4. Taming and Controlling Monkey Mind -9

5. Tackling Disturbing Thoughts Using Micro-Practices-12

6. Managing Unwanted Thoughts -15

7. Correcting Negative Thoughts-17

8. Managing Intrusive Thoughts-21

9. Managing Angry Thoughts- 24

10. Allow the Disturbed Mind to Be-28

11. Living peacefully and happily-30

Part Two – The Mindful Path: Embracing the Present Moment for Peace and Clarity

12. What Is Mindfulness? -36

13. Mindful Living-42

14. Mindful Studying-46

15. Studying Mindfully to Strengthen Retention of Study Material-50

16. Overcoming Performance Anxiety with Mindfulness Practice -53
17. Focus vs. Diffuse Mode-55

18. Overcoming Mental Clutter-59

19. Living in the Present is True Living-63

Part Three-Embracing the Self: A Journey Towards Self-Compassion

20. Self-care-67

21. Love Yourself: Set Aside the Right Time for Yourself -73

22. Be Friendly with Your Inner Self-76

23. Self-Acceptance -79

24. Self-Help Actions-83

25. Developing a Self-compassionate Mindset-87

26. Extend Self-compassion toward yourself, when? -91

27. Master Tips and Tools to Grow in Life-93

28. The Yin and Yang of Self-Compassion-98

Part Four: Navigating Life's Challenges: The Path to Worldly Wisdom

29. Time Management: What & When-101

30. Learn to Adjust and Adapt-109

31. Motivation -112

32. Overcoming Obsession-117

33. Avoid Toxic Persons-119

34. Managing Anger -123

35. Maintain Balance in Life to Aspire for Good Mental Health-129

36. Seize Opportunity or It Will Fly-132

37. Empower the Weak -134

38. Charity Wrapped in Dignity! -136

39. Enjoy the Rhythm of Nature-138

40. Maintain Quality of Life-141

41. Concentrate on True Quality-143

42. Grow Up Actively-146

43. Live a Purposeful Life-148

44. Happiness-153

45. Making Connections -Kintsugi Style-156

46. Social Support-158

47. Our Journey Together Is So Short-161

48. Be a Real Hero-163

49. Focus On Positive -165

50. Overcoming Stress and Anxiety- Vedic Approach -166

Part 5: Spiritual Orientation

51. What Is Spirituality? -170

52. Be a Person of substance and spiritual Orientation-174

Part Six: Words of wisdom and values from Shrimad Bhagavad Gita

53. About Shrimad Bhagavad Gita-180

54. Symbolic Significance of the Chariot Image in the Shrimad Bhagavad Gita -181

55. Some Lessons from the Gita -182

56. How Relevant Is the Bhagavad Gita in Today's World? -222

Epilogue-224

Bibliography-226

About the Author-231

ACKNOWLEDGMENTS

I am deeply grateful to my beloved granddaughter Ishanvi, whose insightful discussions about various issues and persistent exploration of life's challenges inspired me to delve deeper into the intricate workings of the mind. Her inquisitive nature and unwavering curiosity have been a constant source of motivation and enlightenment throughout the writing of this book.

My heartfelt appreciation goes to my esteemed colleagues and students for their invaluable feedback, which has played a pivotal role in shaping the ideas presented in this work. Their contributions have been instrumental in the development of this manuscript.

I am especially thankful to my husband for his unwavering encouragement and support throughout this journey. His belief in my endeavors has been the cornerstone of my strength and resilience.

I owe a debt of gratitude to my children Amit and Meeta for their continuous encouragement and valuable suggestions, which have enriched the content of this book. Their perspectives have added depth and clarity to the concepts explored within these pages.

To all those who have contributed in ways big and small, directly or indirectly, to the creation of this book, I offer my sincere gratitude and appreciation. This work would not have been possible without your collective influence and support.

INTRODUCTION

Welcome to "Taming the Monkey Mind: Mastering Your Thoughts for Inner Peace and Personal Transformation." In this self-help book, we will embark on a transformative journey to understand and tame the restlessness of our minds. The book is a humble attempt to guide youngsters to live purposeful lives. The content of the book is meant to address the complete self of individuals, alluding to their body, mind, emotions, and spirit, in totality. The book is divided into six parts.

The first section of "Taming the Monkey Mind" takes the reader on a life-changing adventure to comprehend and control the restless and frequently chaotic nature of the mind. Perhaps you've experienced the endless stream of thoughts that seem to dart from one branch to another, never granting you a moment of respite. But fear not, for this book is here to guide you on the path to reclaiming control over your mind and finding peace within.

Part two of the book, "The Mindful Path: Embracing the Present Moment for Peace and Clarity" will empower the reader to cultivate mindfulness and unlock the profound benefits of living in the present. In our fast-paced, modern world, it's all too easy to get caught up in the whirlwind of thoughts, worries, and distractions. We often find ourselves living on autopilot, constantly chasing after the future or dwelling on the past, without fully experiencing the richness of the present moment. Within the pages of this book lies the key to rediscovering the power of mindfulness.

Part three is devoted to the topic of self-compassion. "Embracing the Self: A Journey towards Self-Compassion" aims to empower readers to cultivate a kinder, more compassionate relationship with themselves.

Part four of the book, "Navigating Life's Challenges: The Path to Worldly Wisdom "aims to instill practical wisdom in readers. While knowledge is readily available at the tips of our fingers, the application of that knowledge in a wise and discerning manner truly sets us apart. This part of the book is a guide to understanding, developing, and embodying the timeless concept of worldly wisdom.

The fifth part is about spiritual orientation. This part of the book emphasizes that we are not only mind, flesh, and bones. We have spirit also. The viewpoint offered by spirituality suggests that there is more to life than just what people can physically and sensory experience, something greater that connects all beings and to the universe itself.

Readers are introduced to some shlokas from Shrimad Bhagavad Gita in the sixth part of the book. Written thousands of years ago, its teachings offer valuable guidance on various aspects of life, personal growth, decision-making, and attaining fulfillment. For young individuals who often face ethical dilemmas in personal and professional domains, the Gita offers timeless principles to guide their conduct and make choices aligned with their values.

As you embark on this mindful journey, remember that it's a practice- an ongoing commitment to yourself and your well-being. Each chapter will offer guidance, insights, and practical exercises to support you along the way. Read the chapters of the book sincerely. By the time you read the last page of the book, I'm sure you'll be an improved version of yourself.

Let your journey begin!

Madhu Sharma

Part One
Taming the Monkey Mind: Mastering Your Thoughts for Inner Peace and Personal Transformation

1. Taming the Monkey Mind

"The concept of monkey mind represents most people's everyday mental marathon— both the conscious and unconscious consent we give to our minds to bounce from place to place, screen to screen, and conversation to conversation."

The concept of the monkey mind originated from Buddhism. Yogis use the phrase to refer to a mind that jumps from thought to thought like a monkey, that jumps from tree to tree. The monkey mind is unable to be in the present moment but rather is constantly distracted by the thoughts that go through in our mind.

Monkeys are frequent visitors to our garden. They cannot decide what to eat. They keep on jumping from guava tree to papaya tree. From there to the mango tree to pluck leaves. They eat less and destroy more. The same is the state of our mind.

The Buddha introduced the idea of the monkey mind almost 2,000 years ago. He compared the human mind to a bunch of "drunk, inebriated monkeys" that are always fighting, shrieking, chattering, diverting, and overall causing mental havoc. People who struggle with anxiety disorders, stress, or other problematic mental habits can attest to the fact that it frequently feels as though our minds are at war with us.

Fear is a particularly audible and disturbing aspect of this. This negative emotion may be very crippling, whether it's dread of what might go wrong, fear of the unknown, or worry that what we have done in the past will harm us in the future.

There are more distractions than ever in today's fast-paced, technologically enabled society, making it particularly challenging to concentrate on work and study. The constant stream of breaking news from around the globe, which unnecessarily raises anxiety levels for many individuals, makes this situation worse.

Tomorrow is your Physics paper. Your mind is not at peace because of disturbing thoughts that are haunting your brain.

"I could not do well in my previous exam.

Some chapters were not clear to me.

I don't have good notes to prepare.

I won't be able to do well.

Shipra was discussing me with Rajendra.

Why? What can be the reason?

If I am not able to do well, I will not get admission to a good institution."

Endless thoughts haunt you and plague your mind. For this reason, mastering the art of mind control and taming the restless mind is essential. Take a break from continual distractions, decide what matters most to you, and concentrate on the things you can control. The subsequent chapters will embark you on the journey of taming your turbulent monkey mind.

2. Create Conditions for Creativity

Allow "Eureka Moments" to enter your mind.

A statue of Archimedes in a bathtub demonstrates the principle of the buoyant force. Located at MedTech, Israel's National Museum of Science, Technology, and Space in Haifa. (Image credit: Andrii Zhezhera/Shutterstock)

One of the oldest and most well-known legends revolves around Archimedes' fabled "Eureka!" moment while taking a bath in a tub when he made a stunning discovery that is now known as the Archimedes Principle. Archimedes is said to have been so happy, elated, and ecstatic about this finding that he leaped out of the bath and sprinted through the streets to inform the monarch, yelling aloud "Eureka! Eureka!". I have found it! I have discovered it! I am delighted.

The story goes like this. King Hieron II of Syracuse in Sicily gave a goldsmith a bar of gold to turn into a crown after assuming the throne. The king was doubtful after the goldsmith gave him the crown made of pure gold. The monarch thought that the goldsmith had kept some gold and mixed in some inexpensive silver. The monarch, who was unable to corroborate his suspicions, then ordered Archimedes to examine the crown to verify whether it was made of pure gold. He informed the king that he would need some time to think about it.

One day, while he was concentrating on this problem, he decided to take a bath in a tub full of water. He immediately noticed that the water splashed out of his bathtub onto the floor the moment he stepped into it. This triggered an idea that would help solve the king's dilemma. "When I got into the tub," Archimedes reasoned, "my body displaced a lot of water. Now, there must be a relationship between my volume and the volume of water that my body displaced—because if I weren't so big, less water would have spilled on my floor."

Archimedes questioned- what if he put the crown in water? How much water would it displace? And could he apply this to prove that the crown was made of pure gold? He realized that the crown's density was the key. Archimedes already knew that gold was denser than silver. He first took a piece of gold and a piece of silver with precisely the same mass. He dropped the gold into a bowl filled to the brim with water and measured the volume of water that spilled out. Then he did the same thing with the piece of silver. Although both metals had the same mass, silver had a larger volume; therefore, it displaced more water than gold. That's because silver was less dense than gold. So, he realized that if a certain amount of silver had been substituted for the same amount of gold, the crown would occupy a larger space compared to an identical amount of pure gold. He then reasoned that if the goldsmith had indeed made a crown of pure gold, then the volume displaced should be the same as that of a bar of pure gold of the same mass.

Now it was time to check out the crown. To find out the crown's volume, Archimedes immersed the crown in a bucket filled with water to the brim and measured the volume of the spilled water. Then he took a bar of pure gold of the same mass and compared the volume of spilled water to determine if the crown was made of pure gold. He was surprised to note that the numbers were different! The crown displaced more water than the piece of gold. Therefore, the crown's density was less than pure gold. So, indeed the king had been cheated by the goldsmith. You can probably guess what happened to the goldsmith!

Archimedes could make the stunning discovery because his

mind was free. How many of us can keep our minds free? There are several factors at play in today's society that make it more difficult to regulate the monkey mind. Our mind is always busy because it is overloaded with breaking news, desired and undesired thoughts, and stressful moments.

People today frequently juggle many jobs daily, and since technology is always available to us wherever we are, we never have to be bored. Our mind is always occupied by facts, and opinions we are receiving on our mobile or PC. Our brain is never free. Some say we are never bored.

However, there are advantages to being bored!

The environment for extraordinary bursts of creativity, imagination, and elevated states of being can sometimes be triggered by moments of boredom when your mind is free.

Have you ever had a "Eureka!" moment?

Perhaps you've been working on a problem or a concept but nothing seems to be working. Then, later, while you're playing, organizing your cupboard, or finishing another routine chore, an unexpectedly amazing thought or solution appears.

The eureka moment will come only when disturbing thoughts are not troubling us. So, keep your mind free. There can be advantages of a free mind also. Create space in your mind for the "Eureka Moment".

3: Let Us Learn to Live Amicably with Our Furry Friends

We all have a monkey's mind. Despite its light-heartedness, this analogy in reality has a lot of merit. Take into account that we have 6,000 separate thoughts per day as humans, many of which are about the same thing. You could picture that each thought is a branch and our conscious mind is a monkey, 24 hours swinging from one thought branch to another. This goes on day and night.

Source: https://neurosciencenews.com/thought-worms-16639/

A study conducted in 2022 at Queen's University revealed amazing facts about our thoughts. According to the findings of the study, the average person thinks more than 6,000 times every day. Researchers have established a method for the first time, that can detect indirectly when one thought ends and another begins. Dr. Jordan Poppenk (Psychology) and Julie Tseng, a master's student, developed a method to identify "thought worms," which are periods when a person is preoccupied with the same concept repetitively. This research was recently published in *Nature Communications*.

"What we call thought worms are adjacent points in a

simplified representation of activity patterns in the brain. The brain occupies a different point in this 'state space' at every moment. When a person moves onto a new thought, they create a new thought worm that we can detect with our methods," explains Dr.Poppenk, who is the Canada Research Chair in Cognitive Neuroscience. "We also noticed that thought worms emerge right as new events do when people are watching movies. Drilling into this helped us validate the idea that the appearance of a new thought worm corresponds to a thought transition."

Brain imaging scans were employed in the research, which included 184 participants with an average age of 29 years, to monitor the emergence of fresh ideas while subjects were either sleeping or watching a movie. Why did they decide to present movies to participants? They clarify, that those transitions between scenes in movies cause "thought worms," or observable patterns of brain activity, which operate similarly to naturally occurring thoughts. Researchers can tell when one idea finishes and the next begins because every new thought produces a new "worm."

They discovered a median rate of roughly 6.5 thought transitions per minute after testing these transitions at various times on two distinct days. Based on this rate of 6.5 transitions per minute, the researchers estimated that the average young adult would have more than 6,000 thoughts every day as they came to their study's conclusion. (Craig,2020)

Based on their estimation, the math is as follows: Let's say you sleep for eight hours every night. Every day, you spend 16 hours awake and think 6.5 times every minute. (6.5 x 60 x 16 hours) Naturally, this is-

Per minute: 6.5 thoughts

Per hour i.e., 60 minutes: 6.5x60=390

Every day you are awake for 16 hours: 6.5 x 60 x 16=6,240

We all contend with an incessant internal dialogue, commonly referred to as the inner voice, mental chatter, or the monkey mind. Its unceasing activity can be incredibly draining. Many of our thoughts reoccur, evoking feelings of anxiety, hope, and a range of other emotions. The relentless stream of thoughts leaves us feeling worried, stressed, and fatigued. Rather than attempting to rid ourselves of the monkey mind, why not strive to befriend it? Let's explore how we can coexist with and regulate our monkey minds in the following chapters.

Source of image: Internet

4. Taming and Controlling Your Monkey Mind

Co-exist Peacefully with Your Furry Friend

The monkey mind is our natural companion. It is our natural partner. We have to learn to tame it and keep it on our side. Monkeys keep on jumping from one branch of the tree to another. Similarly, thoughts in our minds keep on changing priorities. This is particularly true about students.

Several thoughts occur in the mind of a student. "Should I study or spend time on the basketball court, go to a movie, chat with friends, prepare a presentation, or cover the chapter on Physics?" This disturbs their peace of mind. The issue is that we can neither fight nor subdue the monkey. We can, however, accept it, tame it, and live in harmony with our furry friend. The monkey feels heard and understood and our mind is calm. The Buddhist perspective recommends "Through understanding of the Monkey Mind, the monkey feels like he is being listened to, and understood."

If you calmly and slowly reason out the worries of your mind the mind will not be troubled.

Techniques to be used when the mind is overactivated

When our monkey mind is over-activated, we have to learn the skill to remain calm by using the technique that suits us.

Physical exercise: Physical exercise soothes our minds. The endorphin rush of physical exercise such as running quietens the monkey mind. Endorphins are neurotransmitters that are released by the brain to alleviate pain and promote pleasure.

Yoga: Yoga exercises help. Yoga is a mind-body activity that combines physical movement with an inwardly oriented attentive focus on awareness of the self, the breath, and energy. Yoga combines a person's physical, mental, and spiritual aspects to enhance physical and mental health, especially disorders brought on by stress.

Reasoning: When our mind is clouded, weighing the benefits and drawbacks of a particular action or way of thinking might help us reason with ourselves. Let's live in the present and approach the day by loving the journey we are taking.

Relocate focus from the mind to the body: Moving meditations like Tai Chi and Qigong are other ways to harmonize with the monkey mind. Tai Chi is a healing/martial art that combines martial arts movements with breathing, stretching, and Qi-vital energy circulation procedures. Similar to Tai Chi, the qigong exercise involves a sequence of breath practices combined with bodily movement and meditation to achieve a state of deep focus and relaxation. To put it simply, qigong exercises are performed or employed to improve the harmony and balance of vital energy in the human body. Numerous scientific studies back up the advantages of Tai Chi and Qigong for health.

After all, it takes some practice for us to sit still and not think. These internal arts enable us to use our physical forms to cultivate the intrinsic calm of the soul since the focus is shifted from the mind to the body. (Wang,2017)

We have to learn to live amicably with the monkey mind. We have to be aware that it exists, it will always remain. Let us make sure that it does not define us. Reason with your mind so that frequent movement of the monkey mind does not cause you suffering. If we are conscious of the Monkey's presence, it does not possess us and does not rule us.

Source of images: Internet

5. Tackling Disturbing Thoughts Using Micro-Practices

Let disturbing thoughts be the temporary tenants in your mind

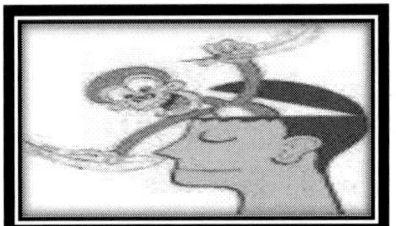

In our day-to-day life, we often have unpleasant and disturbing thoughts. Don't judge such thoughts. Judging means forming an opinion or conclusion about a disturbing thought. Judging solely will become trouble when we make unnecessary, hurtful, or unfair judgments primarily based on little evidence.

Accept and Recognize Disturbing Thoughts

Never pass judgment on a troubling idea or emotion. Instead, accept it and recognize it. Thoughts are just thoughts. They are not always grounded in reality. They might be the result of some previous experience. Therefore, keep in mind that you are not who you are because of your disturbed thoughts. Don't allow such distressful thoughts to have a hold on you. You are not required to keep them. Let them arrive and go. Imagine being on your terrace while witnessing a large group of people and vehicles pass by on the street below. So are disturbing thoughts. They keep flooding our minds.

Let us analyze the impact of disturbing thoughts.

You have to appear for a job interview. Earlier also you appeared for the interview and you were rejected. Disturbing thoughts are coming into your mind.

"I may be rejected this time also.

I badly need this job.

I have to repay the study loan that I have taken.

With no job in hand, I am a burden on my parents."

One after another such thoughts are troubling you. What should you do?

Tackle disturbing thoughts using micro-practices.

Investigate and Analyze: If you feel upset and disturbed investigate the specific reasons behind your disturbing thoughts, their causes, and possible solutions. Why this is happening to you? What can you do to help yourself? Here in this example, your previous failure is upsetting you. Tell yourself everyone faces such situations. You are not the only one.

Non-identify: Release or let go of any thoughts, feelings, or sensations that are no longer helpful to you without judgment.

Set a goal to control your ideas and emotions in a non-judgmental manner. Be aware of your judgments' sources and the circumstances that lead to them. For instance, judgments may be made based on the behaviours and attitudes of those closest to you or based on how they reacted to events or your earlier experience.

Here, your experience of failure and desperate need for the job is triggering unpleasant thoughts. Shun them, and be positive about your capabilities. Tell yourself, that negative, unpleasant thoughts are a natural part of living. We all get hundreds of such disturbing thoughts. Don't allow a bundle of disturbing thoughts to upset you. Everyone experiences such thoughts. They will go away. They are temporary tenants in your mind. Leave them behind and move on.

Source of images: Internet

6. Managing Unwanted Thoughts

"We are what our thoughts have made us; so, take care about what you think. Words are secondary. Thoughts live; they travel far." - Swami Vivekananda

Source of image: Internet

Unwanted thoughts are upsetting and cause frustration. Maybe you don't want to think about failure or a failed relationship. You feel you failed to manage your most prized project or your team lost because of you. You want to get rid of such troubling thoughts that constantly plague and haunt you.

Are you alone and feeling the pressure of unwanted distressing thoughts? You are not alone. We all face similar situations. The following strategies can help change your mindset.

Accept and Recognize Troubling Thoughts

Humans naturally want to avoid suffering and unpleasantness. But staying away won't make our situation better. If ignored, painful thoughts become more intense. Accepting these thoughts is the better course of action. Allow them to come in. Recognize the source of your anxiety.

Think about your mistakes and identify them so that you can avoid them in the future. You could even tell yourself that you made an effort. Maybe you'll perform better the next time.

Try meditation

Meditation helps to develop the practice of tolerating undesirable thoughts. You'll notice that practicing meditation gives you more mental control. Imagine you're trying to focus on a peaceful scene, but suddenly, thoughts about a test you have to take start buzzing in your head. It's like they're trying to steal your attention away from the calm feeling you're trying to create. But with meditation, you learn to handle these thoughts when they come and then let them go, like gently releasing a balloon into the sky. The more you practice this, the easier it becomes to ignore these bothersome thoughts. Eventually, they won't bother you as much, and you'll feel more peaceful and in control of your mind.

Positive Self-talk.

Your mindset can be changed with positive self-talk, but how you speak to yourselves also matters. It won't make much of a difference if we talk about ourselves in the first person. Change your perspective to that of a third person. You can count on it. As opposed to saying:

"I feel miserable because the team lost because of me."

Consider this:

Instead of sulking, "Oh, I'm such a failure," try something like, "Hey you, the team's secret weapon! You've been the star player all along, and the team is lucky to have you. Chin up, superstar, let's turn this setback into a killer training montage. You've got this, champ!"

See, giving yourself a pep talk like you're the MVP of your own story can turn even the toughest defeats into inspiring comeback tales. Give it a whirl, and who knows, you might just score big in the game of life!

Changing your perspective tricks your mind into perceiving you as someone else, providing you space from your difficulties. This is also useful for encouraging yourself because people prefer to take outside assistance more readily than internal encouragement.

7. Correcting Negative Thoughts

Negative thoughts like, "I am not lucky like others, I am good for nothing, I am a total failure, nobody cares for me, I am not needed, and bad things always happen to me only." There is an endless list of negative thoughts that occur in our minds. These can be controlled if we understand how these disruptive thoughts occur and how they can be restructured.

If your thought process is dominated by negativity, if you have harsh thoughts about people, circumstances, and even yourself you're doing yourself a disservice.

What problems are triggered by negative thinking?

When you think negatively, you start to feel bad about the world, about yourself, and about the future. It aggravates low self-esteem. You begin to believe that you are ineffective in the world.

Negative thinking is associated with obsessive-compulsive disorder (OCD), chronic worry, anxiety, and depression, according to psychologists. It results from the structure of our brains. Our limbic system and amygdala are designed to detect hazards and safeguard our survival. Even if the mangrove area in the Sundarbans was gorgeous on a prehistoric day, humans were conditioned to recognize the threat of a predator as it approached. Even when there are limited physical risks today, the same area of our brain is active.

The dangers we face now are primarily mental; they have to do with our preparation for the subject, our income, our ability to find love, and our professional success. That is why we can panic on a Saturday night just thinking about work or our job.

Negative thoughts can be disastrous like a forest fire. These can be controlled if we understand how these disruptive thoughts occur and how they can be restructured. How do we control the forest fire to avoid chaos and destruction? Sensors are installed around the boundaries of the forest. These sensors keep a constant eye on the area's temperature and carbon concentration. Regularly, a thorough report is delivered to a controlling center for monitoring the fire.

Similarly, let us recognize the symptoms of negative thoughts like:

You are not able to concentrate.

Your mind is thinking about past disturbing situations.

Negative thinking can have a spiraling effect

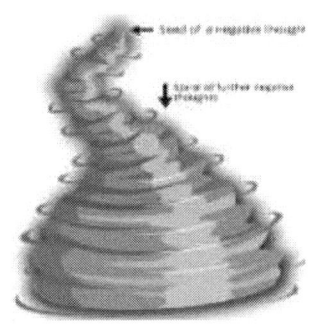

Correction of Negative Thoughts

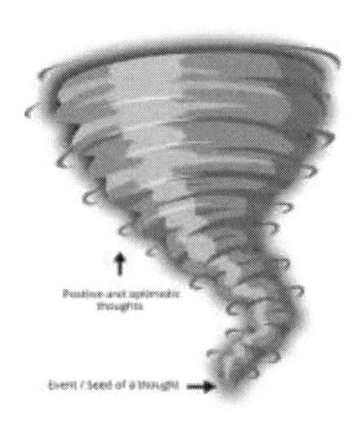

Imagine you have a bad thought, like "I'm not good enough." This thought is like a small seed in your mind. Then, something happens that makes you feel even worse about yourself, like making a mistake at work. This is the trigger that makes the bad thoughts grow. Soon, more negative thoughts start piling up, like "I always mess things up" or "I'll never be successful." These thoughts get stronger and stronger, making you feel even more down. It's like a tornado of bad thoughts swirling around in your head, pulling you away from reality.

But here is the good news: you can stop this tornado. By recognizing these negative thoughts and changing them to something positive, you can turn the tornado right side up. You have the power to break the cycle and feel better about yourself. (Pinchard,2020)

Correct Negative Self-Talk: We all do self-talk. It is often negative also. But the good thing is, we can correct it. Imagine your boss telling you to send a report for the team meeting, you might start thinking, "What if the boss doesn't like it? They might even take away my project, and I could end up losing my job." These negative thoughts keep going in a loop.

This thought process can be corrected. If you think positively. "Sending reports for team discussion is just a regular task. It's an opportunity to share ideas for improving things, which can benefit both the company and me. There's always room for growth and progress. Let's do this!"

Your mental attitude determines how you perceive the world. Think of it like wearing coloured glasses that change how you see everything. If you're always wearing negative glasses, it can affect how you see your health, work, and even your family. What's more, this negative view can keep getting worse, making you see more and more bad things. But here's an encouraging news: we can train ourselves to see things in a better light over time, kind of like learning how to switch to clearer glasses. It takes practice, but it's doable! We have to gradually educate ourselves to think better over time by using basic techniques.

Gain Control Over Negative Thinking

Deal with Negative Thoughts: Spend 10 minutes daily specifically thinking about and analyzing negative thoughts. Write them down and promise to address them during this time. This practice helps you gradually regain control over negative thinking.

Replace with Positivity: Identify negative thinking patterns and consciously replace them with positive thoughts. Focus on a project you're excited about, redirecting your thoughts toward that when negativity creeps in. Expressing gratitude and appreciation also helps.

Ask Tough Questions: Challenge your negative thinking by asking yourself difficult questions. Reflect on the benefits and costs of your negative and positive thought patterns. Understanding their origins and making a plan for the future is essential.

Use Affirmations: Start your day with a smile and gratitude. Create a list of positive affirmations and recall past successes to counteract negative thoughts. Regularly practicing positive thinking can significantly improve your mindset and overall well-being.

Life is beautiful when we learn to manage our negative thoughts because it allows us to find joy and appreciation in the small moments. As we develop the ability to steer our thoughts towards optimism and hope, we open ourselves up to greater possibilities and experiences, allowing us to savor the beauty and richness that life has to offer.

8. Managing Intrusive Thoughts

Intrusive thoughts are unexpected images or thoughts that seem to just appear in your head. They are often unusual or upsetting. But practically everyone has had these thoughts at some point.

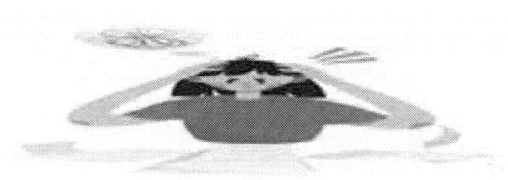

Unwanted intrusive thoughts frequently contain sexual, violent, or otherwise undesirable images. People who have unwanted intrusive thoughts worry that they could in reality carry out the imagined actions. They worry that these thoughts mean something terrible about them. Something is wrong with them. Some unwanted intrusive thoughts consist of:

- vicious, sensual, or socially deplorable images
- repeated uncertainties about relationships
- decisions big and small
- sexual orientation or identity
- thoughts about religion, safety, or death
- questions, and concerns about topics that cannot be answered with clarity
- weird thoughts that make no apparent sense

These are some examples of unwanted intrusive thoughts. Some are merely strange ideas that don't seem to make sense. Unwanted intrusive thoughts can be extremely explicit, and many people keep them a secret because they are ashamed and worried about them.

These thoughts feel extremely hazardous. This happens because nervous thoughts start to dominate, and although the notion may be vile, it does not have any power. People frequently make hasty, hurried attempts to suppress their thoughts, which ironically increases their intensity. Thoughts become more ingrained the more one tries to distract oneself from them, divert them, or try to replace them.

People who experience intrusive thoughts need to develop a new relationship with their thoughts, understanding that sometimes their contents are unnecessary and irrelevant and that everyone occasionally has strange, odd, inappropriately violent ideas.

People who struggle with these thoughts find it tough because they feel helpless. Our minds generate random thoughts, described as the "flotsam and jetsam of our stream of consciousness" – essentially, debris in our stream of consciousness. These meaningless thoughts are like junk. They vanish and are swept away in the flow of consciousness if you don't pay attention to them.

The more one engages with unwanted thoughts, worries about them, fights them, or tries to rationalize them away, the more they will persist. Just ignore these thoughts, soon they will pass away. Treat these as if they aren't even interesting. Just tell yourself, "That's simply an annoying idea; It is not what I believe; It is not what I want to do."

Managing Intrusive Thoughts: Managing intrusive thoughts can be challenging, but with the right strategies and techniques, you can learn to cope with them more effectively. Here are some steps to help you manage and reduce intrusive thoughts:

Practice Mindfulness: Mindfulness can help you stay grounded in the present moment, reducing the power of intrusive thoughts.

Challenge negative beliefs: Intrusive thoughts often involve irrational or exaggerated fears. Challenge these thoughts by asking yourself if they are based on evidence or if they are simply automatic reactions. Consider alternative, more balanced perspectives on the thoughts. Ask yourself, "What is the evidence for and against this thought? "Reframe such thoughts. When you notice an intrusive thought, reframe it in a more positive or neutral light. For example, if you have a thought like "I'm a terrible person," reframe it as "I'm not perfect, but I'm working on improving myself." Use positive affirmations to counteract negative thinking patterns.

Limit exposure to triggers: If certain situations or stimuli trigger your intrusive thoughts, try to limit your exposure to them or develop strategies for coping with them. For example, if watching violent news stories triggers distressing thoughts, limit your exposure to such news or develop a plan for how to handle it.

Talk to someone: Share your intrusive thoughts with a well-wisher, trusted friend, family member, or therapist. Talking about your thoughts can provide relief and help you gain the right perspective.

Remember that managing intrusive thoughts is an ongoing process, and it may take time and practice to see significant improvement. Be patient with yourself and keep working on these strategies to regain control over your thoughts and reduce their impact on your life.

Source of image: Internet

9: Managing Angry Thoughts

"For every minute you remain angry, you give up sixty seconds of peace of mind." - Ralph Waldo Emerson

A young boy had an extremely nasty temper. He used to lose his temper very often. His father wanted to teach him a lesson. He gave him a bag of nails and told him that every time the boy lost his temper, he had to hammer a nail into the fence. On his first day, the youngster hammered 37 nails into the fence.

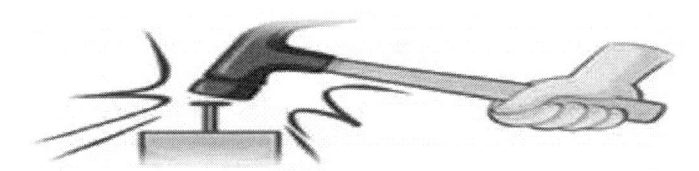

Over the next few weeks, the boy gradually learned to control his temper, and the number of nails he hammered into the fence decreased. He discovered that controlling his temper was easier than hammering those nails into the fence. Finally, a day came when the boy did not lose his cool. He told his father the news, and his father suggested to the boy that he should now pull out a nail every day to keep his temper under control. After a few days, the young boy was finally able to tell his father that all of the nails had been removed. The father took his son's hand and led him to the fence.

"You performed nicely, my son, but look at the holes in the fence. The fence will never be the same again. Things you say in a fit of rage cause wounds like this one."

Moral of the story:

Avoid saying things to people in a rage that you might later regret and learn to control your wrath. There are some things in life that you cannot undo.

"The man who gives way to anger, or hatred, or any other passion, cannot work; he only breaks himself to pieces, and does nothing

practical. It is the calm, forgiving, equable, well-balanced mind that does the greatest amount of work."- Swami Vivekananda

Anger is a natural emotion. Some amount of anger is healthy but like every other emotion, extreme emotion is damaging.

How to Control Anger

"The reason why we have two ears and only one mouth is that we may listen the more and talk the less." — Zeno

Find the root cause of anger.

Analyze what triggered your anger and make an advance decision on how to handle the situation. What makes you angry? Try to get rid of that first.

Address anger timely

If anger is ignored for a prolonged period, it will spiral out of control. Unrest at work is an example of this. If labour dissatisfaction is not addressed promptly, it may flare up.

Avoid spending time with irritating and aggressive people.

Moods are contagious. Avoid spending time with irritable and aggressive people. The company of calm and pleasant people will be beneficial.

Our ability to be creative can help us relax.

Fine arts and music do not make us angry. An angry mood cannot exist in a serene mind. Take up whatever hobby soothes your temper or learn to play an instrument.

Manipulate the environment

Instead of environments that irritate you, seek out ones that are attractive to the eye. Look for settings with pleasing hues. Our moods may be impacted by environmental influences.

Avoid Arguments

Try to avoid arguments when you're sleepy, tired, or hungry as you'll be more prone to irritability, which can quickly turn into fury.

Self-deprecating Humour Helps

This kind of humour can help create a more relaxed and inclusive atmosphere, showing your ability to laugh at yourself and not take yourself too seriously. However, it's important to ensure that the humour doesn't undermine your credibility or competence in the workplace.

Try Postponing Tactics

Postpone your response. You can practice cognitive distance, or "delaying" your response, by going for a walk, using the restroom, or doing anything else that will take you away from the scenario.

Alter your physical state to alter your thoughts

Change your body to change your thoughts, slow down your actions, soften your voice, and adopt a calm demeanour.

As the Stoic philosopher Epictetus reminds us, anger takes us down to the level of a savage beast, petty and malicious, and can destroy the very foundation of who we are by taking control of our emotions and our ability for reason. *"Anger, if not restrained, is frequently more hurtful to us than the injury that provokes it."* - Seneca the Younger

Anger is a harmful emotion that leads us to behave in ways that go against our values, morals, and beliefs. It undermines our true selves, causing us to deviate from the person we aspire to be and the life we aim to lead. This internal conflict often results in destructive, unethical, and immoral actions. Anger can be like a temporary loss of reason. It's advisable to steer clear of anger to maintain a positive course in life.

Source of image: Internet

10: Allow the Disturbed Mind to Be

Buddha once travelled from one town to another with a few of his disciples. They happened to pass by a lake while travelling. They stopped to rest. Buddha told one of his disciples, "I am thirsty. Please bring me some water from the lake."

The disciple made his way up to the lake. When he reached, he noticed that some people were washing their clothes in the water, and just then, a bullock cart began crossing the lake. As a result, the water became extremely muddy and dirty. The disciple pondered, "How can I give Buddha this muddy water to drink?" So, he returned and told Buddha that he could not bring water as it was muddy, and not fit to drink.

After half an hour, Buddha asked the same disciple to go back to the lake and bring some water to drink. As directed, the disciple went back to the lake. This time, the lake's water was crystal clear. The mud was settled, and it appeared that the water was drinkable. So, he gathered some water in a pot and carried it to Buddha.

Buddha looked at the water, then up at the disciple and said, "See what you did to clean the water. You just let it be... and the mud settled on its own, leaving you with clear water..." That is also true of turbulent minds. When the mind is disturbed, simply allow it to be. Give it some time. It will eventually settle down on its own. You don't have to work hard to calm it down. It will occur.

There are times when we feel things are not moving as per our wishes. We need to exercise some patience. With time everything will settle.

What did Buddha emphasize in this story? Having peace of mind is not a difficult task; it is a simple process. When you are at peace within, it permeates the outside world. It spreads around you and in the environment so that others begin to feel that peace and grace.

"So let the mind flow like water. Face life with a calm and quiet mind and everything in life will be calm and quiet."

— Thich Thien-An

Source of image: Internet

11: Living peacefully and happily

The five-letter word PEACE is the most required in our day-to-day life

Where to find peace is a thousand-dollar question.

Places that are associated with inner peace are snowclad high mountains and sea beaches where people are relaxing. It is very nice if someone has resources and time to go to places in search of tranquility but all of us are not blessed with loads of money, and facilities. We have to find peace living in crowded places with all the stress of life. We need inner peace in our day-to-day life while standing in a long queue of groceries waiting for our turn, boarding the local train or bus, or walking in the crowded market. This chapter will suggest ways and techniques regarding how to live happily and peacefully without going to high mountains or living the life of a saint sitting on the bank of a river to find inner peace.

Look Inside Yourself

Were you always like this, an agitated, short-tempered person with frowns? No. We are born with the gift of inner peace. As a young child, this is reflected on our face-a smiling, frown-free face, that always used to gleam even with small possessions- a coin, pebbles, coloured paper, a wire, etc.

Peace and Serenity Can be Acquired by "Micro Practices"

Peace of mind, that is hiding within us can be accessed and acquired by "micro-practices"

Think of the Bottom of the Sea

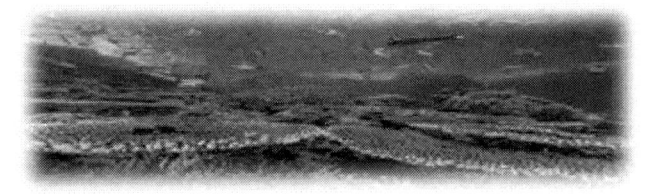

The bottom of the ocean is a glaring example of tranquility.

The surface of the ocean is disturbed by the constant movement of waves but a few meters down, there is a serene world of creatures moving at their pace, completely undisturbed by the action up above. Your inner self is peaceful. You are designed that way.

There is no living being in the world who is free of day-to-day ups and downs. We are not always successful. We have rough patches in life, in relationships. If we can develop skills of "micro-practices", we can live peacefully. "With the help of what Bush calls "micro-practices," you can get better at accessing your inner calm—even if it's been in hiding for a while."

Rhythmic breathing in, and breathing out can help us.

You may be disturbed because of the nonstop flow of disturbing thoughts. Try natural treatment given to all of us by generous God-breathing in and breathing out!

Breathing exercises can alter our mental state. They are encouraged in both yoga and meditation practices. Here's a simple exercise:

Count to four as you take a deep breath through your nose. Hold your breath for the count of seven. Then, exhale slowly through your mouth for a count of eight. The prolonged exhale encourages the parasympathetic nervous system, which is primarily starting your body's relaxation response. (Our parasympathetic nervous system is a network of nerves that relaxes our body after periods of stress.)

Think You Are Alive, You Are Breathing.

Another skill is to feel that you are breathing, you are alive, you have people around you, and you can connect with them during turmoil.

Visualize Happy Moments

Another powerful micro skill is the visualization of happy moments. Go back to your past happy memories, and childhood days. Think about the places that gave you happiness and peace. Reminding yourself of sweet smells, sounds, and scenery will elevate your disturbed mood and you will experience tranquility. Visualizing the moment when you won your first race, you sang on the school stage, the presentation for which you were appreciated, such memories will lift your mood.

Adopting RAIN Technique

The RAIN technique is a reflection procedure, based on the old Buddhist practice of mindful meditation. Initially conceptualized by Michele McDonald, RAIN is an abbreviation for Recognition, Acceptance, Investigation, and Non-Identification. This technique detaches us from our disturbing thoughts and emotions and helps us to find peace and tranquility.

What is the RAIN Technique?

RAIN technique can wash away our self-judgment and self-analysis, leaving us euphorically washed in self-empathy and self-esteem.

In nature, how do we feel after rain? Imagine, you are in your garden in hot weather. Plants are covered in dust and lose their luster. What happens after rain? All dust is washed away. The plants look very green. Same way RAIN Meditation technique washes away the dust of disturbing thoughts.

Basic Steps of Rain Technique

R: Recognize

What is going on in our mind and its effects on our body? Life is a battleground where we are constantly interacting with the environment, surroundings, and people. By recognizing what is happening to our minds and bodies at such times, we can identify the reasons for our pressure and make plans to improve things.

A: Accept

Accepting the thoughts and feelings that come up is another micro-practice. Thoughts are thoughts. At times, our thoughts are not always based on reality. They are shadowed by our previous experience.

I: Investigate

Look into what you are going through with mild curiosity. When a lot of negative thoughts are running through your head, it might be difficult to make sense of the world. In these circumstances, ask yourself questions about what you are experiencing. This can improve your understanding of the world and your situation and help you discover and find the joy of living. Investigate the specific reasons behind your overwhelming feelings, their causes, and possible solutions if you feel overwhelmed.

To investigate ask yourself questions:

What is disturbing me and why? On which part of my body, I am feeling strain- heart, mind, neck, or shoulder? Can putting my hand gently on these parts will help me? Do these inquiries gently with love not like a heartless investigator as you need to calm down.

N: Non-Identify

Allow yourself to release any thoughts, feelings, or sensations that don't help you anymore. Try not to be hard on yourself as you do this. Think about why you're being hard on yourself and what's making you feel this way. Sometimes, it's because of how the people around you act or react to things you do. (Roy, 2022)

RAIN can assist you in being more detached from your thoughts and feelings while increasing your awareness of them. Regular use of it might make you a close friend of yourself and bring your thoughts into a more serene state.

God has blessed us with inner peace. Let us try to master the techniques that suit us to live peacefully. It is not difficult.

Source of images: Internet

Part Two – The Mindful Path:
Embracing the Present Moment for Peace and Clarity

12. What is Mindfulness?

"Mindfulness is a love affair—with life, with reality and imagination, with the beauty of your own being."
—Jon Kabat-Zin

Imagine this: you're standing at a bustling intersection, thoughts racing, worries piling up like an insurmountable heap, and the cacophony of modern life drowning out the whispers of your own existence. Now, picture a magical key that unlocks a door to a tranquil garden of the mind, a place where every breath steadies your thoughts and every moment is savoured with a profound sense of awareness. Welcome to the captivating realm of mindfulness, a transformative practice that invites you to be fully present, embrace each second with intention, and uncover the profound peace that resides within.

Mindfulness involves keeping a calm, peaceful, and compassionate awareness of our thoughts, feelings, physical sensations, and surroundings on a moment-by-moment basis.

Also, acceptance is a component of mindfulness. Acceptance includes noticing our thoughts and feelings without criticizing them—without, for instance, assuming that there is a "right" or "wrong" way to think or feel at a particular time. When we practice mindfulness, our thoughts are directed toward the present moment rather than reliving the past or the future. Mindfulness has its roots in Buddhist meditation. It has both physical and mental benefits.

In our day-to-day lives, we act in a way we never intended. Someone crosses us, overtakes us from the wrong side, and we lose our cool and patience. We feel impatient with our relatives, and family members and react frustratedly. All these are mindless activities. In the end, we are surprised how can we react like that. Such situations can be avoided if we push ourselves to practice mindfulness for just a few minutes at different times during the day.

Mindfulness is an awareness

According to Jon Kabat-Zinn, well-known author and founder of the Stress Reduction Clinic at the University of Massachusetts, "Mindfulness is an awareness that arises through paying attention, on purpose, in the present moment, and non-judgmentally."

Mindfulness changes the way we interact with people and situations. It cultivates a broader, less reactive, and overall happier way of being in the world. The following story will explain mindfulness to us.

Once Lion, the king of the jungle summoned all the animals of his kingdom and shared his plan to entertain everyone. He said that every day he would nominate one animal of the jungle to narrate a story to fellow animals. The rule is that the animal has to narrate a comical story and make everyone laugh. If the narrator can make everyone laugh, he will be rewarded with the best food of his liking. But, if he fails to make others laugh, he will be punished and banished from the kingdom.

First of all, the fox was given the task of telling the story. The fox was smart and sharp and was known for her sense of humour. The story was hilarious. Everyone laughed and laughed except the donkey. Unaware, he kept on grazing. The story had no impact on him. The king was furious. He asked the fox to immediately leave the forest.

The next day, he changed the theme of the story. He decided that the narrator would narrate a sad story that should move everyone. He gave this task to deer. The deer was very nervous. Then he told his own story. He had a difficult childhood after the death of his mother who was killed by the hunter. Everyone was moved. Tears were flowing from the eyes of all. Even the lion was moved but everyone was startled when the donkey was laughing and laughing.

The king roared and asked the donkey why was he laughing.

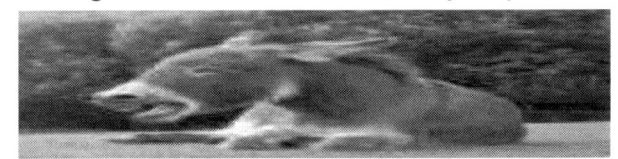

The donkey explained, that he thought of yesterday's story and started laughing. As per the rule, the lion banished the deer because he failed in the task. One animal was not moved by the story.

If we analyze the story, we reach the following conclusion:

- The tiger was not mindful. He punished without realizing that the donkey could not process the story.
- The donkey was not self-aware. His reactions were slow. He was thinking of the past instead of being in the present. When everyone was laughing, he was eating grass, and when everyone was sad, he was laughing. He was not present at the moment. He was thinking of the past. Both lacked mindful wisdom.
- The king realized his mistake and revoked his order. He called back both the fox and the deer.

Mindfulness is the practice of becoming more fully aware of the present moment—non-judgmentally and completely—rather

than dwelling in the past or projecting into the future.

What happens when we are not mindful?

I am presenting three situations:

Situation 1- You come to your mathematics class after your sports period or after the break when you have enjoyed yourself with your friends. You are not able to focus in the mathematics period as you are too excited about the previous experience.

Situation 2- You feel anxious and nervous because of your past negative experiences. You did not read the paper correctly or you copied the wrong number or you committed mistakes as you were not attentive, and your mind was somewhere else. The memory of such experiences disturbs you. Fear is there in your mind. In such situations, you will find it difficult for a moment to focus on the paper before you.

Mindfulness and awareness of the present moment will help here.

Try Mindfulness Minute

One of the most straightforward methods you may use to help yourself or someone else overcome anxiety is the concept of a mindfulness minute. A mindfulness minute helps to concentrate and makes us conscious of our feelings and actions. In a mindfulness minute, there is a variety of exercises we can employ so here are some strategies to help you structure a mindfulness minute:

- Close your eyes for one minute and count your inhales and exhales for a count of four to six. This technique allows students to focus on their breath. You will feel calm and composed.
- Be aware of the present moment and let all the stress of thoughts go away. Like Arjun saw the eye of the fish only. Arjun was able to shoot accurately because he meant business and focused on the goal only, while his brothers were distracted by the environment and other objects.

- Close your eyes and notice and appreciate the silence or the natural sounds of the classroom.
- Close your eyes and repeat a mantra to yourself that follows your breath. Gayatri mantra can be recited.
- In a seated position, with your legs crossed, close your eyes and think about relaxing the muscles on your face.

It only takes a minute to incorporate mindfulness into a classroom or exam room, but the results have a huge influence on the student's health, performance, and well-being.

Mindfulness is different from our default mode

Developing steady and non-reactive attention is frequently diametrically opposed to how we are in the world. Many of us spend a considerable portion of our lives on autopilot, completely unaware of what we are doing and missing out on all the sights, sounds, fragrances, connections, and delights we could be experiencing. Some of the time, our minds appear to be "switched off," while others are wrapped up with ideas from the past (including regrets) or future goals, most of which are repeated.

Imagine you're at a beautiful beach, watching the waves crashing on the shore. However, your mind is preoccupied with thoughts about a disagreement you had with a friend earlier that day. You're not really seeing or feeling the beauty of the beach because your mind is stuck in the past.

Now, let's say you start practicing mindfulness. You take a moment to acknowledge your thoughts about the disagreement, but then you gently bring your focus back to the present moment—the sound of the waves, the feel of the sand beneath your feet, and the salty breeze on your skin. As you do this, you begin to feel more connected to the beauty around you and less tangled up in your past thoughts and worries.

By practicing mindfulness, you're able to enjoy the present moment more fully, without letting past events cloud your experience. This helps you to respond to situations more calmly and thoughtfully, rather than reacting impulsively based on past experiences or future concerns.

Compare your default mode with a mindful state

Consider your reaction when you don't believe you're good at something, such as completing brain teasers. What do you do when you're given a mental teaser during an interview? Do you tell yourself, "I am not good at this," or "I am going to look stupid"? Is this causing you to lose focus while working on the puzzle?

How would it be different if you approached it with an open mind, with no concern or judgment about performance, simply an interest in working on the brain teaser?

Simply being fully present in the moment and accepting everything that happens, internally as well as externally, without passing judgment is mindfulness. Being present and aware of everything around you are exactly the opposite of daydreaming, which involves switching off and letting the default mode network kick in and take over. The candidate started solving the puzzle he was asked to solve without being affected by his past experience or worrying about the future outcome. He lived in the present moment and solved the puzzle.

Source of images: Internet

13. Mindful Living

What is mindful living?

"Do not dwell in the past, do not dream of the future, concentrate the mind on the present moment."- Gautam Buddha
This quotation has beautifully summed up mindful living in a few words.

Developing Mindful Habits

We live in a fast-paced world where there is no time "to stand and stare." Demands continue to come in from various areas of life, keeping us busy. There is no time for us to even smell the jasmine or roses in the garden. We try to acquire that from the perfume bottle. The moment has come to practice mindful living because there are times when we need to slow down. We may enhance our pleasure, joy, and sense of purpose in life by practicing mindful living. Being mindful, however, is not as easy as it sounds. It is a habit that has to be developed.

Habits to be more mindful

Mindful morning habit establish proper mindset

Start each day in the right frame of mind. The early morning offers an excellent opportunity to start the day mindfully. The day is just getting started, it's peaceful, and you might have some time to yourself. Sit for a while in the morning rather than hurry through your morning ritual after getting out of bed. Enjoy the peace of the early morning, such as the birds perched on the pole, the distant sound of someone chirping, the low sun's red beams coming from the blue sky, and the smell of the soil. Try to be grateful for the day and try to stay in the moment. You can either opt to meditate or simply sit on the couch and focus on regulated breathing. All of this contributes to establishing the proper mindset each day.

Eat mindfully

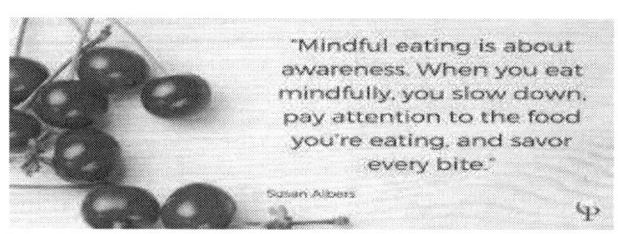

> "Mindful eating is about awareness. When you eat mindfully, you slow down, pay attention to the food you're eating, and savor every bite."
>
> Susan Albers

We eat food as if it is a routine like another routine. Do we ever appreciable meals or do we just eat because we have to eat? Shun the habit of munching, and gulping food because you have to eat. Eat purposefully, and enjoy each bite of food, fully enjoying the smell, texture, and aroma of food. This will improve your digestion. Meal time should be the most relaxing time for you.

Wrong practices during the meal time

- Avoid distractions while eating.
- Discussing or watching violence/politics
- Eating with eyes on mobile
- Texting or surfing while eating
- Eating amidst unpleasantness

Put down the smartphone and enjoy the moment of the meal. Have you seen the group of labourers eating during a thirty-minute lunch break? They sit in a circle, share, and eat what they bring in their tiffin box happily being present in the moment. They may not have the luxury of a great variety of food, expensive dining tables, and a bulk of knowledge but they have the luxury of relishing food and mindful eating. Eating the right food at the right moment and in right manner is mindful eating.

Spend some time outside

Another technique to practice mindfulness is to spend some

time outside; you don't necessarily need to travel to a remote retreat, hill station, or a foreign country to see and feel the benefits of time spent outside. Simply going for a walk around your community would do. The ideal setting for reconnecting with nature and the present moment can be created if you have some lovely trails, parks, or green places. While out on a stroll, pay attention to what you see, how the weather feels, what you hear, and what you smell.

Meditation helps

Meditation can be thought of as the practice of mindfulness. You are giving yourself some time to spend with your mind when you meditate. The benefits of controlled breathing are numerous, but it does take some time to practice them and block out all of the outside distractions. It may be a terrific time for relaxation and stress alleviation in addition to being a time for awareness.

Do one task at a time

Many of us have the myth that we are multi-tasking and can perform many tasks together efficiently. They feel that taking on as many chores as one could was the most effective strategy. It is almost instinctive to think that doing more at once is better, but this is untrue. You are not giving any of the tasks the attention they require if you divide your attention among several of them. In reality, research has shown that multitasking increases the chances of mistakes more likely and takes longer than performing the job independently.

Focus on the work at hand and complete one task at a time. After finishing, take a brief break before starting the next assignment. It is a more leisurely and deliberate way to complete tasks, and it certainly will improve your performance.

Feel all shades of feelings comfortable uncomfortable both

You shouldn't push your feelings away when practicing mindfulness. Being in the now, being in the present exactly as it is, is a big part of it. There may even be instances when you experience delight, but you shouldn't try to suppress your emotions or think only of positive things. Sometimes you simply have to accept uncomfortable feelings as a part of the present. Allow yourself to experience disappointment, sadness, wrath, envy, etc. as they are. You should pay attention to how you respond to the feelings, but it is also beneficial to accept them for what they are. Your dear ones are not well, many leave us. That is part of life. Accept that.

Have a creative pastime

This might be a great chance to practice mindfulness if you have a creative pastime. Spend some time enjoying yourself while remaining present in the act of creating. Another thing is that mindfulness training can boost creativity. Many people have found that practicing mindfulness is an effective approach to rekindling their lost creativity. You might discover that fresh, original ideas come to you more readily while you're walking or meditating and when your mind is free. Grab those ideas.

Mindful physical activity

It is easiest to be mindful when we are engaged in an activity that we enjoy and that needs both our body and mind to pay attention. For instance, in cycling, basketball, badminton, or trekking, you can miss your aim or get tossed around if you lose your focus while doing these activities. Finding something you like to do will allow you to spend time entirely absorbed, which will help you learn how to apply mindfulness to other aspects of your life.

These are just a few practices that can help to be more mindful, but many different things will work for different people. You'll have a new sense of power over your life when you are more mindful and in the moment. You'll be able to discover lasting satisfaction in the long run.

Source of images: Internet

14. Mindful Studying

Creator: Tatiana Smirnova

How do we view learning?
A pleasant activity or a hostile activity?
In their book, *"The Mindful Way to Study"*, Jake and Roddy Gibbs point out that a lot of the phrases we use to describe studying are pretty violent — we're going to "hit the books," "nail the test," or "hammer it into our heads." What do these expressions convey? We don't like to study.

Don't View Learning as a Battle

Instead of viewing learning as a battle — you vs. the content, view it as a relationship. It's you and the material like colours and your creation on canvas. If you are passionate about music, you are immersed in music. Let us compare learning to dance, where the dancer interacts with the music. Ballroom dancing is a cooperative activity, not a combative one. Let learning be a joint venture, not a battleground between you and books. Let there be no hostility between you and the study material.

What stimulates you?

What motivates you to study?
Do you want a 10 CGPA /A+?
What motivates you at your workplace?
A pay hike/promotion in office?

While grades and money are important, if they are your primary reason for learning something, you will likely learn less and like it less. Similarly at the workplace, if your only aim is a pay hike or promotion, you will be always under pressure, and will not enjoy your work.

In a well-known study, two groups of kids were given free access to a choice of toys. The first group was just permitted to play with whichever toys they wanted. The second group was given the same instructions but was also compensated for utilizing the toys. Which group did you think had more fun with the toys? The kids that were paid to play. This guess is wrong. No, because the extrinsic incentive diminished the intrinsic enjoyment of the exercise. It's like when you're playing just for the fun of it, and then someone adds rules that take away the joy.

Our performance declines as we place more emphasis on the results of the activity than on the actual process. Consider the contrast between your performance during a practice of badminton where no one is watching and your performance during a competition when all eyes are on you. Your coach often tells you to concentrate on the game, on the technicalities of the game not on the result of the match. Similarly, while studying, concentrate on the understanding of the content, enjoy the subject material, and avoid all distractions like grades, opinions of others, and future worries. You and the learning material, or your work should be the best friend.

Take Cognitive Break

Give your brain a break! After about forty minutes of focused work, it's good to take a pause. You could take a short walk, grab a snack, or play with your pet before getting back to your book or task.

Keep Changing Your Study Locations

It is beneficial to study in different locations. When we study in different locations, we pick up a variety of additional clues from our surroundings. To store that information, we develop new neural networks in our brains. You do recall solving a similar calculation while working outside while that colourful peacock appeared on the terrace. You read that story while curled up on your favorite sofa in the study.

Try Interleaved Practice

Throughout our educational journey, we've often been instructed to focus on one subject at a time. In school, we'd have dedicated time for math, literature, or science, diving deep into a specific topic before moving on to the next. This method is known as "blocking" or "massed practice."

Even though it might be conventional, studies suggest that distributing our learning and varying the topics we cover in each session is more effective than focusing on just one skill at a time. Instead of learning about a subject all at once or over the course of a week, spaced learning involves returning to a subject at regular intervals over a few weeks or months. The benefits of "distributed practice," often known as spaced learning, have been well-established. Students who stretched out their learning compared to those who studied the same subject in blocks remembered 10% more information, according to a research on 254 students.

Interleaving, also known as "interleaved practice," comes in, as combining various study techniques into a single study session enables students to cover a lot of material in a brief period.

What is the benefit of interleaving?

However, studies suggest that mixing up our learning and alternating the topics in each session can be more effective. Imagine learning a new language, where instead of spending hours on just vocabulary, you also practice speaking, reading, and listening in each study session. This technique, known as "interleaving," can boost your overall language proficiency more rapidly than studying each aspect separately.

Similarly, in sports training, instead of focusing solely on perfecting one move, incorporating various drills and exercises during a single practice session can help improve overall performance. For instance, a soccer player might practice dribbling, passing, and shooting consecutively, rather than spending a whole session just on shooting practice.

The key is to allow the brain to make connections between different skills or subjects, enhancing your understanding and retention. While it might seem challenging at first, interleaving can lead to a more comprehensive grasp of various concepts and skills, making your learning experience more enriching and effective in the long run.

Imagine you're studying. You might spend some time on Mathematics, then switch to Chemistry, and later focus on Physics. Then you might go back to each subject again, but in a different order, using different ways to study. This helps your brain make connections between different subjects. For example, you might see how something you learned in Physics is related to what you just studied in Math

To enhance their learning, students can blend or interleave different subjects or topics while they are studying. On the contrary, blocked practice involves studying one subject matter in great detail before going on to another. Researchers feel that interleaving is more successful than blocking practice for developing the skills of categorization and problem-solving abilities. Interleaving also boosts long-term retention as well as the transfer of learning of learned concepts. Each practice attempt differs from the last, therefore this method requires the brain to constantly retrieve because rote replies drawn from short-term memory won't work. Interleaving, according to psychologists strengthens memory associations and the brain's capacity to distinguish or discriminate between concepts.It's important to study each topic thoroughly and give yourself enough time to understand it well. But remember, switching subjects shouldn't be a way to avoid a tough topic. Instead, try to stick with it until you feel you've really got it. (https://academicaffairs.arizona.edu/l2l-strategy-interleaving)

15. Studying Mindfully to Strengthen Retention of Study Material

Do you forget what you have learned?

Don't worry. It is normal.

In reality, forgetting is a crucial component of learning. You might complete your homework on Monday and review what you've learned all week on the weekend. The information you read on Monday has been forgotten. Kind of. You retrieve the data once more for examination. You make the brain's information-storing neural networks stronger.

It will be interesting to learn about the neural networks. Neurons are the basic building components of your brain. We all have about 100 billion of them, and each one can link with 250 000 neighbouring neurons because they are information senders and receivers in your brain. And, if neurons are the transmitters, neural pathways are what provide meaning to the information they communicate to our brains.

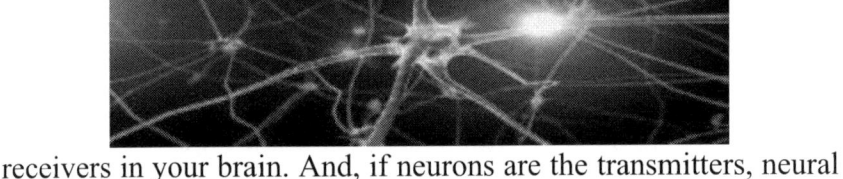

How neural pathways can help in overcoming the problem of forgetting and improve memory retention

Neural pathways play a significant role in both forgetting and remembering information. To overcome the problem of forgetting and enhance memory retention, you can leverage the principles of neural pathways in several ways:

Repetition and Practice: Repeatedly engaging with the information you want to remember strengthens the neural pathways associated with that knowledge. Regular review and practice help prevent these pathways from weakening over time. This is known as the spacing effect or spaced repetition, and it's an effective strategy for long-term retention.

Elaborative Encoding: When you learn something new, try to connect it to existing knowledge and create associations. This process, known as elaborative encoding, helps build more robust neural pathways. The more connections you make to the new information, the easier it is to retrieve later.

Chunking: Divide complex information into smaller, more manageable chunks. This strategy reduces cognitive load and allows you to focus on strengthening specific neural pathways associated with each chunk. It's particularly helpful for remembering long strings of information, such as phone numbers or passwords.

Visualization and Imagery: Creating vivid mental images related to the information you're trying to remember can enhance memory. Visualization and imagery techniques engage multiple regions of the brain, reinforcing the neural pathways associated with the content.

Use Mnemonics: Mnemonic devices are memory aids that involve creating associations between new information and familiar concepts. Mnemonics help build stronger neural pathways for memory retrieval. For example, acronyms, rhymes, or acrostics can be useful.

Sleep: Quality sleep is essential for memory consolidation. During sleep, the brain reinforces and strengthens the neural pathways related to the day's experiences and learning. Aim for adequate and regular sleep to optimize memory retention.

Stress Reduction: Chronic stress can impair memory and weaken neural pathways. Implement stress management techniques like meditation, deep breathing, or exercise to reduce stress and support better memory function.

Healthy Lifestyle: Maintaining a healthy lifestyle with regular exercise and a balanced diet can positively impact brain health and the strength of neural pathways. Physical activity, in particular, has been shown to promote neuroplasticity (the ability of the brain to form and reorganize synaptic connections).

Multisensory Learning: Engage multiple senses when learning new information. Combining visual, auditory, and tactile inputs strengthens neural connections associated with that information.

Teaching and Sharing Knowledge: Explaining what you've learned to someone else or teaching it to yourself reinforces your understanding and the corresponding neural pathways. This is known as the "protégé effect." (The *protégé effect* is a psychological phenomenon where teaching, pretending to teach, or preparing to teach information to others helps a person learn that information)

Mindfulness and Concentration: Practicing mindfulness and deep concentration when learning can help you create stronger neural connections for the material. Minimize distractions and immerse yourself in the subject matter.

Review and Retrieval Practice: Periodically quiz yourself or review the material without looking at your notes. The act of recalling information strengthens the associated neural pathways and makes it easier to remember in the future.

By applying these strategies, you can harness the power of neural pathways to improve memory retention and overcome the problem of forgetting. Keep in mind that individual differences exist, and what works best for one person may vary from another. Experiment with different techniques to discover the most effective memory-enhancing strategies for yourself.

16. Overcoming Performance Anxiety with Mindfulness Practice

Overcoming performance anxiety through mindfulness practice can be a valuable tool for students and professionals alike. Mindfulness is the practice of being fully present and engaged in the moment without judgment. When applied to academic situations, it can help reduce anxiety, improve focus, and enhance overall performance. Here's an explanation with an example:

1. **Understanding Performance Anxiety**:
Performance anxiety often occurs when students or professionals are faced with tasks such as exams, presentations, or public speaking. It can manifest as physical symptoms like a racing heart, sweaty palms, and a racing mind, which can hinder one's ability to think clearly and perform at his best.

2. **Mindfulness Practice**:
Mindfulness involves techniques such as deep breathing, meditation, and body scans to help individuals stay grounded. By practicing mindfulness regularly, individuals can develop greater self-awareness and control over their reactions to stressors.

Example: Preparing for an Academic Presentation
Let's consider an academic scenario where a graduate student is preparing for a crucial presentation at a conference. This student has a history of performance anxiety. Here's how mindfulness can help:

Mindful Breathing: Before the presentation, the student takes a few minutes to engage in mindful breathing. He focuses on his breath, inhaling deeply and exhaling slowly. This helps calm his nervous system and reduces physical symptoms of anxiety.

Present Moment Awareness: Instead of worrying about potential mistakes or how he will be judged, the student practices being fully present at the moment. He reminds himself that he has prepared for this presentation and that he is knowledgeable about the topic.

Body Scan: The student does a quick body scan, checking for any physical tension. He consciously releases tension in his shoulders, neck, and jaw, allowing his body to relax.

Acceptance and Non-Judgment: Throughout the presentation, if the student notices his mind wandering or negative thoughts creeping in, he acknowledges them without judgment and gently brings his focus back to the topic at hand.

4. Results:
By incorporating mindfulness practices into his preparation and presentation, the student is more composed, focused, and less affected by anxiety. He delivers a confident presentation, and his ability to articulate ideas is greatly improved. This not only helps him overcome performance anxiety but also enhances his academic performance.

In summary, mindfulness practice in academia can be a powerful tool for overcoming performance anxiety by promoting self-awareness, calming the nervous system, and fostering a more focused and present mindset. By incorporating mindfulness techniques into their academic routine, students and professionals can enhance their overall performance and well-being.

17. Focus vs. Diffuse Mode

When we study or learn some skills there are moments when our productivity is very high. We experience a "flow state." We tick off our to-do list successfully. When you easily block out distractions, you are in focused mode. We would love to be in this mode forever if possible! But this does not happen.

According to Barbara Oakley, we now understand that in order to produce our best work, we must transition from a state of productivity to a more relaxed one. We alternate between focus mode and diffuse mode throughout the day.

Look at the chess match depicted in this image. Observe the young man to the left. He is competing with the player to the right. The youngster is an ordinary 13-year-old boy. He is Magnus Carlsen. He even left the room to look at other games during the competition. The other player is Garry Kasparov one of the best chess players in the world. It appeared to people who were watching this game that Magnus is not paying attention; thus, he cannot possibly succeed. Right? It's amazing that Kasparov lost the chess match. It was a tie. The best chess player in the world couldn't win against a thirteen-year-old who seemed to be perpetually distracted. Surprise! We occasionally need to become distracted in order to think more clearly. Zoning out can be helpful sometimes (but not always).

During the game, Magnus left the table but quickly returned and refocused on the game. He had a brief rest so that when he returned, he could concentrate better.

The takeaway from this story is that sometimes being less focused helps you learn more effectively. How is that possible? It is possible.

You can think in two ways! To better understand the brain and to peep inside it, neuroscientists are using cutting-edge brain-scanning equipment. Your brain functions in two distinct ways, according to neuroscientists. These two methods of operation will be referred to as the focused mode and the diffused mode. Remember, both models are helpful in learning.

Focused Mode: Your focused mode indicates that you are paying attention when you are in it. You might be attempting to solve a math problem, for instance. Or perhaps you're listening to your teacher's lecture. Playing video games, putting puzzles together, or learning words in a foreign language all need concentration. You activate specific brain regions while you are focused. Which parts are working depends on what you're doing. Your brain will use different regions to focus when you're solving multiplication problems than when you're chatting, for instance.

How does the learning process start? You must first concentrate hard on the concept in order to "turn on" certain portions of the brain and begin the learning process when attempting to learn anything new.

Diffuse Mode: Your mind is comfortable and free while it is in diffuse mode. You aren't considering anything in particular. When you're daydreaming or drawing for enjoyment, you're in diffuse mode. When your instructor asks you to focus, you have probably entered diffuse mode. When your brain is in diffuse mode, it is gently using additional areas that are typically not used when you are focused. You may develop more creative connections between concepts when you use the diffuse mode. Utilizing the diffuse mode seems to often promote creative thoughts. (Oakley,2018)

It is observed that our brain has to switch between focused and diffuse modes to learn effectively. So don't worry. When your mind is imagining or when you are day dreaming, there is nothing wrong with you. You are taking a break for better learning. But don't take this break when your exams are close!

Focus and diffuse thinking moments in the context of learning and problem-solving

The concepts of focus and diffuse thinking moments are often discussed in the context of learning and problem-solving. These two modes of thinking can be illustrated with an academic example:

Focus moment during learning:

Imagine a student who is working on a complex mathematical proof. In a focused moment, the student is deeply engaged in the task. He is concentrated on the specific problem at hand, using his analytical skills to follow each step of the proof. This type of focused thinking is crucial for solving intricate problems and understanding intricate concepts in academia.

For instance, in the middle of his proof, the student encounters a challenging equation that requires careful manipulation and mathematical insight. During this focus moment, he dives deep into the problem, perhaps consulting his textbooks and notes, and works through the equation step by step. This focused approach allows him to eventually arrive at a solution or a more profound understanding of the mathematical concept.

Diffuse moment during learning:

Now, let's consider a "diffuse" thinking moment in the same academic context. After hours of intense focus on the mathematical proof, the student may hit a roadblock. He feels stuck and can't seem to make progress on a particular part of the proof. Frustration sets in, and he decides to take a break.

During this "diffuse" moment, the student shifts his attention away from the problem. He might go for a walk, take a shower, or engage in a completely unrelated activity. As he lets his mind wander, he may not be consciously thinking about the proof, but his subconscious continues to work on it in the background.

Then, suddenly, while taking a shower or during a walk, an idea or insight pops into his mind. He realizes a new approach to solving the problem, or he sees a connection between the proof and another concept he encountered earlier. This "aha" moment occurs during the "diffuse" thinking phase when the mind is free to make broader associations and connections.

A student's ability to switch between focused thinking and diffuse thinking is essential for academic success. While focus helps him tackle complex problems systematically, diffuse thinking allows him to gain new perspectives and creative insights that can lead to breakthroughs in his academic work. Both modes of thinking complement each other and are valuable tools for problem-solving and learning in academia.

Source of image: Internet

18. Overcoming Mental Clutter

Oh, the menace of mental clutter, how it sneaks in, uninvited yet persistent, like an unwelcome visitor that just won't leave. It's like a cluttered attic, filled to the brim with random thoughts, worries, and to-do lists, all jostling for attention. Can't seem to find the light switch in this mess. And then there's that constant chatter, the relentless inner monologue that just won't hush. It's like a never-ending radio broadcast, broadcasting worries, fears, and doubts on repeat. How does this impact us, though? How does this clutter and chatter affect our ability to perform, to excel, especially as students, when we're expected to absorb information like sponges and produce results like well-oiled machines?

Let's take a deeper dive into this maze of the mind, shall we?

Let's unravel the tangled web between our thoughts and our academic competence, and discover the ways to overcome this mental commotion that can become a silent yet formidable barrier to our success.

Mental clutter and chatter can significantly impact the performance of students in various ways. Here is an example to illustrate this:

Consider the case of a high school student named Sarah. She has been struggling with multiple personal issues, such as family problems and financial stress. On top of that, she is trying to balance her academic workload, which includes various subjects and extracurricular activities. Due to the constant mental clutter caused by her personal issues, Sarah finds it challenging to concentrate on her studies.

In the classroom, her mind often wanders, making it difficult for her to grasp complex concepts or fully engage in class discussions. Additionally, the constant inner chatter related to her personal problems distracts her during exams, causing her to underperform and achieve lower grades than she is capable of. As a result, her academic confidence diminishes, leading to a lack of motivation and a negative impact on her overall academic performance.

Furthermore, Sarah's mental clutter affects her ability to manage her time effectively. She frequently forgets important deadlines and fails to prioritize tasks, resulting in late submissions and incomplete assignments. This disorganization further exacerbates her academic stress and negatively affects her academic progress.

Moreover, Sarah's mental clutter and chatter also impact her social interactions. She finds it challenging to communicate effectively with her peers and teachers, hindering her ability to participate in group projects and collaborative activities. This isolation further contributes to her feelings of being overwhelmed and unable to cope with the demands of school.

In this way, the mental clutter and chatter experienced by Sarah not only affect her academic performance but also have a detrimental impact on her emotional well-being and overall educational experience. It is crucial for educators and support staff to recognize these challenges and provide students like Sarah with the necessary support and resources to help them manage their mental clutter and improve their academic performance.

How can Sara overcome this mental clutter and regain her academic focus?

Certainly, clearing mental clutter can be achieved through personal efforts. Here are some effective strategies that individuals can implement to declutter their minds and improve their focus and performance:

Mindfulness and Meditation: Practice mindfulness techniques, such as meditation and deep breathing exercises, to cultivate awareness of the present moment and develop the ability to observe thoughts without getting entangled in them. This practice can help in reducing stress and improving concentration.

Journaling: Maintain a journal to unload and organize thoughts, feelings, and tasks. Regularly jotting down concerns and priorities can provide a sense of clarity and direction, enabling individuals to prioritize tasks effectively and reduce mental congestion.

Time Management: Create a structured schedule that includes dedicated study time, leisure activities, and breaks for relaxation. Setting specific time slots for different tasks can help in efficiently managing one's workload and reducing the tendency for distractions to take over.

Physical Exercise: Engage in regular physical activities like exercise or sports to release pent-up stress and boost mood-regulating endorphins. Physical movement can serve as a productive outlet for negative emotions, allowing individuals to clear their minds and approach tasks with renewed energy and focus.

Setting Realistic Goals: Set achievable and realistic goals to avoid overwhelming oneself with an excessive workload. Breaking down tasks into manageable steps and celebrating small achievements along the way can help in maintaining motivation and preventing feelings of being swamped by an unmanageable workload.

Limiting Distractions: Minimize distractions by creating a conducive study environment, free from unnecessary disruptions like electronic devices or loud noises. Implementing techniques like the Pomodoro technique, which involves working in focused bursts with short breaks in between, can help enhance productivity and reduce mental clutter.

Social Support and Communication: Seek support from friends, family, or mentors to discuss concerns and alleviate emotional burdens. Open communication about challenges can provide a fresh perspective and emotional relief, contributing to a clearer and more focused mindset.

By incorporating these personal efforts into their daily routines, individuals can effectively declutter their minds, enhance their ability to concentrate and improve their overall performance in various aspects of life, including academics.

19. Living in the Present is True Living

True living is living in the present. The Sanskrit word "Vartaman," which is also used in Hinduism to denote both living and the present moment, serves as confirmation of this. Additionally, Vartaman refers to the present, as opposed to the past (Bhuta) and future (bhavishya). Living is identical to being in the moment because that is the actual living.

I have come across a beautiful story, posted by Gregory Angel about a man who encountered a ferocious tiger while he was approaching the edge of a cliff, passing through the forest.

The man was getting close to a cliff's edge when a tiger approached. He gripped a vine with both hands since he had to descend. Halfway down the slope, the man saw the tiger at the top of the cliff showing its teeth. He looked down to the bottom where another tiger was growling at him. He was sandwiched between them.

To add to his worries, two mice, one black and the other white, arrived on the vine above him. They started nibbling at the vine. He knew that the vine would soon become too weak to support his weight if the mice kept munching on it. If it shattered, he would fall. He tried to frighten the mice away, but they kept coming back.

He saw a strawberry blooming on the face of the cliff not far from him. It seemed ripe and tasty. He grasped the vine with one hand and reached out with the other, to pluck the fruit.

While a tiger sat above, another below, and two mice continued to nibble on his vine, the man plucked the strawberry and enjoyed its taste!

The main lesson of this story is to live in the moment.

Living in the present is the central theme of this tale. The man decided to remain alert despite his dangerous circumstances. He was able to enjoy and capture the event.

Metaphors in the story

The story's main components are all symbolic representations with deeper meaning. The past is represented by the cliff's peak. It is both the man's past location and the origin of his journey. To ascend the vine and reach the cliff's edge would be to go back in time. The risk of spending too much time in the past is symbolized by the tiger at the top. If we consistently criticize ourselves for not performing particular tasks as well as we ought to have or if we wallow in sorrow and humiliation for errors we have committed, the tiger has bitten us. If we are unable to let go of sad memories from the past that make us fearful and timid, or if we feel like victims due to our traumatic upbringing the tiger has bitten out of us.

Additionally, the tiger stands for the inability to change the past. Sometimes we wish we could go back in time and make certain decisions again. The passage of time is a one-way passage!

The future is represented by the cliff's base. It is the uncharted terrain and the unfinished book. The future has all of your hopes and anxieties, expectations and letdowns, potential successes and potential failures. It is the enigmatic and unknowable world of tomorrow.

As you descend the vine and get closer to the cliff's base, you can gaze ahead, plan for, and make predictions about what is ahead. The bottom-most tiger symbolizes the risk of worrying excessively about the future, especially when it interferes with our capacity to act in the present or to keep peace of mind.

The man is standing in the present, sandwiched between the two tigers. He is hovering in midair, as you can see. Similarly, we also live suspended lives between the past and future.

The present is here, and it is entirely yours. You alone have the authority to decide how to use it, and no one has the right to remove it from you.

But just as the mice never stop returning, time never stops moving and never stops for anyone. Our time in this corporeal world is finite, despite our greatest efforts.

The strawberry is a symbol of the incredible beauty, pleasure, vigour, and vitality of the present. Enjoy the present moment. For those who can see it and experience it, it is constantly there and accessible. So, live in the present moment wholeheartedly. Stick to your plan of action to live consciously in the present. (Angel G.,2017)

Creator: AigulGaraeva   Source of images: Internet

Part 3-Embracing the Self

A Journey towards Self-Compassion

20. Self-Care

A gentle art of loving yourself

We all want to be fantastically healthy and live a long and happy life. However, we may be unaware that every one of us, to a considerable extent, possesses the solution to accomplishing these goals within ourselves. It's called self-care, and it's never been more necessary as we approach the stressful time after the outbreak of the coronavirus pandemic and the Ukraine war.

But what precisely is self-care?

It is the deliberate practice of protecting and improving our own physical and mental health as part of a balanced lifestyle. It has never been more important in these stressful and unpredictable times. Self-care entails the deliberate activities of eating healthily, getting enough sleep, exercising frequently, having a strong social network, caring for our spiritual needs, protecting our financial security, and much more.

It can be difficult to start practicing self-care

Self-care is not always simple to do. Most of us don't have time for ourselves because we are either overworked, have stressful careers, rigorous schedule, have demanding jobs, have many other responsibilities, or are too engrossed in technology. Me-time typically comes last on the schedule. Even worse, we may occasionally feel guilty for sacrificing the time we need to care for ourselves. So, it can be difficult to start practicing self-care.

Self-care keeps you strong, sane, and resilient

It's crucial to understand that when we are talking about self-care, we have to take care of our body, mind, and spirit on a daily basis, not just when we are upset or unwell. Self-care practices such as eating well, managing tension, exercising frequently, and taking breaks, when necessary, can keep you strong, sane, and resilient.

How to stay healthy, happy, and resilient?

It is a thousand-dollar question, and the answer is self-care. Self-care is not always easy to implement. Here are some tips that can help.

Self-care Tips:

Make sleep part of a self-care routine

Sleep can have a huge impact on our emotional and physical well-being. Inadequate sleep can lead to major health concerns. However, worry and other distractions can interfere with our sleep. What can we do to get adequate sleep?

- Do not eat or drink immediately before bed. Stay away from caffeine and sugar, which tend to keep you awake.
- Destress yourself
- Next, make sure your bedroom is the best possible place for you to have deep, dreamless sleep. The room should have thick dark curtains to stop all sources of light when you are sleeping. It ought to be uncluttered. Switch off the television, laptop, and cell phone.

What Are REM and Non-REM Sleep?

While you're sleeping, your body goes through a lot. You alternate between REM and non-REM sleep while you're sleeping.

What is REM?

Rapid eye movement is referred to as REM. Your eyes move quickly in a variety of directions while you are in REM sleep, but your brain is not receiving any visual information from your eyes. Non-REM sleep does not involve that.

The cycle begins with non-REM sleep, is followed by a brief period of REM sleep, and then it repeats. Most often, dreams occur during REM sleep.

What Takes Place During Non-REM Sleep Stage?

Non-REM sleep is divided into three stages. Each step may go on for five to fifteen minutes.

Stage 1: Even when your eyes are closed, it is easy to wake you. up. This stage may last for five to ten minutes.

Stage 2: It is the stage of light sleep. Your body temperature drops and your heart rate slows. Your body is preparing for a restful sleep. That may go on for ten to twenty minutes.

Stage three: This is the stage of deep slumber. It's more difficult to wake you up at this stage. If someone did, you would feel confused and disoriented for a while. This is the most important stage of sleep as, during this stage, the body builds bone and muscle, heals, repairs, and regrows tissues, and strengthens the immune system when in deep periods of NREM sleep.

Make exercise part of your daily routine.

We all understand the benefits of exercise, but do we fully comprehend these benefits? Daily exercise benefits physical and emotional health, improves your mood, relieves stress and anxiety, and helps you lose extra weight. It is not possible to visit the gym every day even simple walking, playing some games, or yoga is equally beneficial.

Right Food: Food has the power to either keep us healthy or add to weight gain or illnesses like diabetes, and hypertension but it also has the power to keep our minds active and awake. Short-term memory loss and inflammation, both of which can have long-term effects on the brain and, in turn, the rest of the body, can be avoided by eating the correct food. To obtain various vitamins and minerals, try to eat a variety of meals. Nutrient-dense foods include green vegetables, fresh fruits, lean meats, whole grains, dairy products, pulses, nuts, and seeds, fatty seafood, blueberries, and brassicas like broccoli. These are some of the best foods for self-care.

Master the art of saying "No": Many of us feel compelled to say yes when someone begs for our time or energy because it is extremely difficult to say no. However, accepting invitations from family members or colleagues when you're already stressed or overworked can cause burnout, anxiety, and irritability. It might take some practice, but once you master the art of saying "no," you'll begin to feel more self-assured and have more time for your own needs.

Take a self-care vacation: A self-care vacation can significantly improve your life. Even if you're not especially stressed out, taking a weekend trip can help you unplug, unwind, and recharge. These excursions for self-care don't have to be expensive; just take a drive to the neighboring town to see the sights or go camping. The idea is to take some time away from your routine and do something for yourself. There is no need to spend a huge sum on change, but some change in daily routine is required sometimes.

Spending time in the open: According to studies, spending time in the open is a wonderful way to deal with depression or burnout symptoms. Going outside can also improve your ability to sleep at night, particularly if you engage in physical exercises such as walking, hiking, or gardening.

Spend some time with pets: Pets bring a boost to our lives. Our lives can be improved by spending some time with pets. Our four-legged friends can be incredibly helpful for our self-care, offering companionship and unconditional affection. Dogs in particular can help decrease stress and anxiety levels.

Become a healthier version of yourself

- Getting organized is the first move to becoming a healthier version of yourself because it enables you to determine precisely what you need to do to take better care of yourself.
- Making a small adjustment, such as pasting a calendar or planner on the fridge, can make it easier for you to keep track of all your obligations, schedules, and meetings while also keeping your life a little more organized.
- Designating a space to keep your keys, wallets, briefcases, backpacks, and coats makes you organized and prepared for the next day, and will make life smoother. You don't have to spend time searching for your things.
- Stay connected with yourself, friends, and well-wishers. Spending time with friends and well-wishers can make you feel more at ease and connected.

Finding spare time can be challenging for all of us.

However, scheduling regular self-care time is crucial. You can stay grounded and think about the best methods to proceed in your life when you are by yourself for a while. Self-care is not self-indulgence, it is self-preservation. "Don't sacrifice yourself too much, because if you sacrifice too much there's nothing else you can give, and nobody will care for you."

21. Love Yourself

Set Aside the Right Time for Yourself

"You are a VIP; a very important person so take care with self-care. If not you, who? If not now, when?" - Toni Hawkins

"Take care of yourself! "This is a typical phrase used to bid a friend or loved one farewell. It's an innocent and kind wish for the people we care about. But do we keep in mind to "take care of ourselves" as well? Not really. We would all benefit from a gentle reminder now and then to prioritize our own well-being. Unfortunately, this "reminder" often comes when we have hit rock bottom or are extremely exhausted in body, mind, or soul.

There are so many cases every day where we see youngsters not taking care of themselves. They fail to strike a balance in life. If you will not take care of yourself, you will perish but the rest of the world will keep on moving. No one will look back or wait for you. So, you better take care of your body, mind, and emotions. Keep yourself physically fit. Keep yourself mentally alert, and nourish your mind and emotions with positivity.

The sayings that are included here are excellent for serving as a constant reminder of the value of caring for oneself, embracing self-care, and learning to prioritize one's own needs.

"When admiring other people's gardens, don't forget to tend to your flowers."

"Self-care is never a selfish act-it is simply good stewardship of the

only gift I have, the gift I was put on earth to offer to others." -Parker Palmer

Making your happiness a priority is not selfish, nor is taking care of and loving yourself. At the end of the day, if we don't first nourish and care for ourselves, we can't be the best for others. "Rest and self-care are so important. When you take time to replenish your spirit, it allows you to serve others from the overflow. You cannot serve from an empty vessel."

Give Time to Yourself

"While too much time alone can lead to loneliness, spending just the right amount of time on your own could benefit your well-being."

"Sometimes Scientists just need to be left alone. Peter Higgs, for example, recently claimed that he would not have been able to complete his Nobel-prize-winning work in the current research environment, stating that the peace he was granted in the 1960s is no longer possible. Einstein, Cavendish, Heisenberg, and Dirac were other isolation-loving researchers."

Alone Me Time/Appreciate Me Time

In the digital world of today, how much time do we give to ourselves- just my time when we have found time to sip coffee/tea leisurely when we have switched off all disturbing devices? We have become slaves of YouTube. Throughout the day we want to see and know what is happening where, as if we are the Secretary General of the UNO, and minute-to-minute reports of Russia-Ukraine war, Israel-Hamas problem should be before us all the time.

One should be aware of what is going around us but not at the cost of our mental peace and emotional well-being. For our well-being let us find alone me time. We will have to develop this habit. This is self-care.

Learning to value "alone/me time" gives us the opportunity and space to develop our creative side. Being alone can help control our emotions. It has a calming impact that makes us better able to interact with other people.

According to a recent article in The New York Times, Durham University assistant professor Thavy Nguyen made an interesting observation about solitude: "We have some evidence to show that valuing solitude doesn't really hurt your social life, in fact, it might add to it."

With this discovery, she gave us a peek at a profound secret: the key to discovering joy is choosing it while accepting loneliness. Learning to value "alone me time" gives you the freedom to explore your creative side and gain a deeper understanding of who you are. Solitude can have a calming impact that makes us better able to interact with other people by assisting us in controlling our emotions. Alone me time at the end of the day or at the end of the week, unplugging all social media, and regular activities energize us. Great feats are achieved by creative writers, artists, and scientists during "alone me" time.

Source of images: Internet

22. Be Friendly with Your Inner Self

"The highest purpose of intellectual cultivation is to give a man a perfect knowledge and mastery of his own inner self."- Novalis

I was on my way to Bombay from Jaipur. It was a long journey. I was concerned about how solitary and bored I would feel for so long. Fortunately, I had a fantastic travel partner, and it was a very relaxing trip. We introduced ourselves and patiently shared our experiences without being harsh or sarcastic. It was a fantastic journey.

We Are Never Alone in Journey of Life

We travel a long road in life. On this trip, we're never alone. Our inner voice or inner self is a continuous companion. We are always talking and visualizing.

How do we handle ourselves?
Are we self-respecting, considerate, and kind?
The response is unfavourable.
Most of the time we are rejecting ourselves.
"I was wrong here.
I could have done better.
I am responsible for the mess of life."
This never-ending monologue goes on and on.

"You can search throughout the entire universe for someone more deserving of your love and affection than you are yourself, and that person is not to be found anywhere. You yourself, as much as anybody in the entire universe deserve your love and affection."- Buddha

Let us be friends with ourselves. We have done the best we could do. In the fantastic journey of life, let us be harmonious in our thoughts and actions. We will be happier if the constant monologue that goes on in our minds is cordial and productive.

How Negative Thoughts Hound Us

I heard the conversation of my friend Pooja over the phone. She was talking with her friend Diva, who could not get a good score in her term examination. These are some excerpts from the conversation.

"Pooja, why are you disturbed?

An examination is also a kind of learning.

We can always improve our performance.

I am sure, with your kind of intelligence, you will crack the final exam with flying colours. You have the potential.

Everything will be all right. If you could not do well in one test; this doesn't mean you will not do well always. The second chance is always there.

Relax

Bye

Take care

Don't worry."

Now imagine how will you behave with yourself in a similar frustrating situation.

"I am to be blamed for everything.

I got the best facility but did not utilize it.

All my friends are doing better than me.

I have wasted my life.

I am a total failure.

My life is no good"

We keep on hitting ourselves and condemning ourselves. This kind of self-criticism is self-sabotage. Mono dialogue of self-acceptance would be; "I have done the best. I can always keep on trying." Self-analysis is life. Self-condemnation is self-assassination. Positive self-analysis is "If I could not do well during my school- college days or in my job, there is no dearth of time. I can always restart. If I have given my hundred percent, if I am doing my work honestly, I am happy and contented. God has given me a beautiful caring family, a good upbringing, good physique, I am grateful to God". The counter remedy for self-rejection is self-acceptance.

23. Self-Acceptance

Self-acceptance is described as "an individual's acceptance of all of his/her attributes, positive or negative." It comprises accepting one's physical appearance, personality traits, preferences, and family background, shielding oneself from negative comments, and having faith in one's abilities.

You must have heard the story of the crow, who was not happy with his looks. Let us revise the story.

A crow used to live happily in the forest. He found himself the most beautiful and always cherished his beauty. One day while he was going in search of food, he saw a white swan. He was stunned to see the dazzling white swan and began to feel depressed since the swan was so white, while he was so black. He complimented the swan for his beauty. The swan said, "A parrot is really lovely and has two lovely colours—green and red."

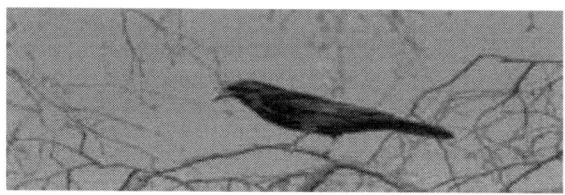

The crow next visited a parrot. He told the parrot, "You are the most beautiful and happy bird I have ever seen." Hearing this, the parrot expressed disappointment and remarked, "You are wrong, my dear friend. I was happy till I saw a peacock. Peacock has the most vibrant colours and is the most attractive bird."

The crow then walked to the peacock to meet him in a zoo. The vibrant peacock mesmerized him, and he concluded there was no bird more beautiful than the peacock. He said to the peacock, "You are so lucky and beautiful, my friend,". Thousands of people visit you every day to admire your beauty. Compared to you, I am so black. No one likes me. "I used to think the same, but I was mistaken" the peacock retorted. "I'm confined to the zoo because of my attractiveness. Crows have always been able to move freely, and because of this, I believe they are the happiest birds in the world. Nobody traps them. So, my dear friend, you are fortunate and happy" the peacock said.

Likewise, many of us find ourselves ensnared in a relentless cycle of discontentment because of our habit of measuring our own happiness against that of others, resulting in feelings of despondency and a belief that others enjoy greater fortune. We never focus and value ourselves. We continue to judge others instead. We never express gratitude for what we have. We should keep moving and keep our attention on ourselves. The moment we start comparing, we start a never-ending race that will never let us become happy.

Two Options

"Option A: Spend your life trying to get others to accept you. Option B: Accept yourself and spend your life with others who recognize what a beauty you are."-Scott Stabile

Point to Remember

"Remember, you have been criticizing yourself for years and it hasn't worked. Try approving of yourself and see what happens."- Louise Hay

How to Nurture Self-acceptance

Nurturing self-acceptance is a vital component of personal growth and well-being. It involves embracing and loving yourself for who you are, with all your strengths and weaknesses. Here's an elaboration on how to nurture self-acceptance:

Practice Self-Compassion: Treat yourself with the same kindness and understanding that you would offer to a close friend. When you make a mistake or encounter a challenge, avoid self-criticism and instead practice self-compassion. Understand that it's normal to make mistakes, and it's an opportunity for learning and growth.

Challenge Negative Self-Talk: Pay attention to your inner dialogue. When you catch yourself engaging in negative self-talk or self-criticism, challenge those thoughts. Replace them with more positive and constructive affirmations. For example, instead of saying, "I'm not good enough," say, "I am doing my best, and that's enough."

Set Realistic Expectations: Avoid setting unrealistically high standards for yourself. Understand your limitations and don't expect perfection in everything you do. Recognize that it's okay to have limitations, just like everyone else.

Embrace Your Imperfections: Nobody is perfect, and that's perfectly okay. Embrace your imperfections as a part of what makes you unique. Your flaws and vulnerabilities make you human, relatable, and authentic.

Self-Reflect and Self-Accept: Take time for self-reflection to gain a deeper understanding of your values, beliefs, and personal history. Acknowledge your past mistakes and experiences without judgment. Recognize that these experiences have shaped you and helped you grow.

Celebrate Your Achievements: Acknowledge and celebrate your accomplishments, no matter how small they may seem. Recognizing your achievements, no matter how minor, can boost your self-esteem and reinforce self-acceptance.

Practice Self-Care: Make self-care a regular part of your routine. Take care of your physical, emotional, and mental well-being. Engage in activities that make you feel good about yourself and nurture your self-worth.

Let Go of Comparison: Comparing yourself to others is a common obstacle to self-acceptance. Remember that everyone's journey is unique, and comparing yourself to others is often unfair and unhelpful.

Be Patient: Nurturing self-acceptance is an ongoing process. Be patient with yourself and understand that it may take time. There will be ups and downs, but the key is to keep working on it.

In short, self-acceptance is about embracing your true self, including your strengths and weaknesses, and recognizing that you are worthy of love and respect just as you are. It's a journey of self-discovery and self-compassion, and by practicing these strategies, you can cultivate a deeper sense of self-acceptance and lead a more fulfilling life.

Know Yourself Be Yourself Accept Yourself

Happiness and self-acceptance go hand in hand; the more accepting of yourself as you are, the more happiness you will enjoy. Along with an increase in positive feelings, a sense of independence, self-worth, autonomy, and self-esteem, these are additional advantages. Self-acceptance reduces depressive symptoms. You believe in yourself and do not feel the need for approval from others. You do not fear failure and are always ready to improve. Nhat Hanh has rightly said *"To be beautiful means to be yourself. You don't need to be accepted by others. You need to accept yourself."*

Source of image: Internet

24. Self-Help Actions

"You are not your yesterday. You are what you make of your todays. Mistakes will happen, don't let that discourage your future. Use your broken thing to make unbroken wings. Then fly."

Self-help refers to numerous actions taken to enhance one's life. Taking breaks, having a positive outlook, and changing the environment are all examples of self-help.

Learning to Control Your Life

The case of a young talented engineering student was in the news. This exceptionally brilliant student got a seat in the prestigious top engineering institute. Suddenly, he changed his line and joined the film industry. He gave a few successful movies and earned fame and wealth. Some of the most poisonous people come camouflaged as friends and family when you become famous and rich. Unfortunately, this young talented person lost control of his life. He became a drug addict; his girlfriend controlled all his wealth and one day he was found hanging from the ceiling fan of his bedroom with an empty bank account. This fellow had no control over his life. A talented life is wasted.

Look outside of yourself for assistance if you want to improve your life to find the root cause of the problem. In this case the person required outside help from medical experts, well-wishers, and true supporters.

We are the root of the majority of our troubles. A significant step towards a happy way of life is learning how to handle these problems. Self-help does not mean giving up control. Instead, it means mastering the ability to reclaim it and possessing the capability to alter our lives when necessary.

Self-help techniques:
Self-Improvement

Improvement of oneself is a lifelong endeavour. It can be as simple as making an effort to eat healthier, substituting fruit for all the sugary cereals in your pantry, working out to lose weight, or developing intricate new routines like meditation. To accomplish that, you must plan and have a strategy. It involves bettering oneself.

Self-Empowerment/ Self Exploration

This involves finding out more about oneself. It is a form of self-discovery, often known as introspection or searching within oneself. We all have our strengths and weaknesses. *"We all make mistakes, have struggles, and even regret things in our past. But you are not your mistakes, you are not your struggles, and you are here NOW with the power to shape your day and your future."* — Steve Maraboli

Making the conscious decision to control your future is the first step towards self-empowerment. Making wise decisions, acting to advance, and having faith in your abilities to make and carry out decisions are all part of it. Self-empowered individuals are motivated to learn and achieve because they are aware of their strengths and weaknesses.

Self-Direction

Self-direction refers to being the captain of your own ship, steering through the unpredictable tides of life, free from the gusts of societal pressures or the undertow of external expectations. This kind of freedom, where you're the master of your fate, is what we call self-governance. It's like having the reins in your hands, deciding what's best for you without getting swayed by the winds of others' opinions.

Think of it as choosing not to board a ship destined for rocky waters even when others insist it's the way to go. This mindset of self-determination can be a lifeline, preventing you from sailing into troubled waters or even the tempting yet treacherous whirlpool of harmful choices like taking drugs under peer pressure. It's like understanding that experimenting with harmful substances, despite their undeniable allure, is akin to knowingly steering your ship toward a storm.

By embracing self-determination, you're not just

safeguarding yourself from future storms, but you're also fine-tuning your present voyage. It's the compass that helps you navigate towards calmer seas and clearer skies, ensuring a smoother journey ahead.

"Positive self-direction is the action plan that all winners in life use to turn imagination into reality, fantasy into fact, and dreams into actual goals." — Denis Waitley

Motivating Oneself

It may seem tough to inspire oneself, but in reality, you all do it every day. You motivate yourself by making decisions and choices, choosing what you want rather than doing things automatically. Self-motivation can help you avoid making the same mistakes twice and, if desired, improve current problems.

Having Positive Thoughts

This entails surrounding oneself with individuals who, despite their challenges, are joyful and full of life because they choose to be positive rather than negative, which makes them feel better about themselves and others around them! Positive individuals are beneficial for your mental and physical health since negativity can lead to depression or sadness, i.e., a less-than-desirable state of mind that leads to feelings of emptiness inside.

Here's a brief true story of self-improvement:

John, a young man in his mid-twenties, was struggling with a lack of direction and purpose in his life. He felt like he was merely drifting, bouncing from one dead-end job to another, and his self-esteem was at an all-time low. This discontentment led him to take stock of his life and embark on a journey of self-improvement.

Identifying Weaknesses: John began by identifying his weaknesses and acknowledging his lack of education, self-discipline, and self-confidence. He was determined to confront these limitations head-on.

Setting Clear Goals: He set specific, achievable goals for himself.

He decided to pursue higher education, enrolling in a part-time college program to earn a degree in a field he was passionate about.

Establishing Healthy Habits: John started a daily routine that included regular exercise, a balanced diet, and adequate sleep. These habits boosted his physical and mental well-being.

Self-Education: He developed a thirst for knowledge and spent his free time reading books, taking online courses, and expanding his skill set.

Mentorship: Recognizing the importance of mentorship, John sought out individuals who had achieved success in their chosen field and learned from their experiences.

Networking: He actively networked and built relationships with like-minded individuals who shared his goals and aspirations. This allowed him to gain valuable insights and opportunities.

Challenging Comfort Zones: John pushed himself out of his comfort zone. He took on new responsibilities at work, volunteered for challenging projects, and sought public speaking opportunities to overcome his fear of public speaking.

Embracing Failure: Instead of fearing failure, John learned to embrace it as a part of the learning process. He treated each setback as a valuable lesson.

Over several years, John's dedication to self-improvement paid off. He completed his degree, secured a job in his desired field, and started to excel. His self-confidence grew, and he began to set even more ambitious goals. This story of self-improvement is a testament to the power of determination, self-awareness, and continuous growth. John's journey serves as an inspiration for anyone looking to overcome personal limitations and achieve their full potential through self-improvement.

25. Developing a Self-compassionate Mindset

We work day and night for success and personal development. This is also true that our society commonly respects people who are self-assured or self-confident when it comes to personal development. We also see many very successful people suffering miserably when they fail. To approach success and personal development, however, self-compassion may be a better strategy. The following passages will confirm this.

For instance, self-confidence makes you feel better about your abilities while self-compassion, encourages you to accept your flaws and limitations along with success as no one is perfect. Furthermore, you are more likely to see your imperfections objectively and realistically once you've accepted and acknowledged them. This, in turn, can lead to positive changes in your life.

Drawn from Buddhist philosophy, self-compassion is different from self-confidence. As opposed to being a method of thinking about yourself, it is a way of being or a way of treating yourself. It is about developing a self-compassionate mindset.

Components of Self-Compassion

According to the writings of Buddhist scholars' self-compassion has three main components:

(a) self-kindness

(b) a sense of common humanity

(c) mindfulness

A self-compassionate mindset is the result of the interaction and combination of these elements.

Self-kindness: Self-kindness is the tendency and ability to treat oneself with compassion and understanding rather than with harsh criticism or condemnation. Self-kindness brings calm and consolation to the self in times of hardship as opposed to adopting a "stiff upper lip" attitude.

When you practice self-kindness, you realize that everyone has shortcomings and that everyone has an imperfect life. And when things go wrong, you are gentle to yourself rather than judgmental and critical. For instance, if you could not crack an entrance test, or could not get the profession of your choice, your initial thought maybe "This should not be happening to me." Or you might think: "Only I am unsuccessful. All my other friends are settled in the field of their choice. They are so happy"

Points to be noted:

You are likely to suffer more when you think negatively or unkindly because it makes you feel alone, alienated, and different from everyone else. However, when you have self-kindness, you think, "Well, everyone fails once in a while," as opposed to, "Poor me." You recognize that everyone faces difficulties and challenges because this is what it means to be human. When you begin to think in that way, it alters how you perceive life's issues and challenges. This allows you to learn from the experience.

A sense of common humanity: Recognizing that suffering, difficulties, and setbacks are universal aspects of the human experience is another vital component of self-compassion. It involves understanding that you are not alone in your challenges;

everyone encounters obstacles and makes mistakes throughout their life. Embracing this shared human condition fosters a sense of connection and reduces feelings of isolation.

You were preparing for the swimming competition. You reached the semifinals but lost in the finals. You think over the matter and tell yourself we don't always win. There are so many others like you who could not reach finals in their first attempt. Your realization that you fell short of swimming skills; and the winner was more skilled will help you improve your skills in the future.

Mindfulness: The third element of self-compassion is mindfulness, which is being aware of one's present-moment experience in a clear and balanced way to avoid ignoring unfavourable parts of oneself or one's life's imperfection. Mindfulness is the ability to observe your thoughts, emotions, and experiences without judgment. In the context of self-compassion, it means being aware of your pain or struggles without overidentifying with them or becoming overwhelmed by them. This component encourages individuals to maintain a balanced perspective on their difficulties, allowing for a more measured and compassionate response to their own suffering.

For example, if the sample prepared by you is not accepted by the company, don't blame yourself, rather find ways to improve the quality of your sample to pass the test next time.

You must also be aware of your inner critic. In the above example, your inner critic could hammer you and could have made you believe that you are unworthy which is why your sample is not accepted. Self-criticism may be very demoralizing and keeps replaying in our minds. But with mindfulness, you may be aware of your shortcomings without berating yourself. You will be able to pinpoint your areas for improvement as a consequence without feeling pressured to be superhuman.

When these three components are integrated into one's mindset, they create a foundation for self-compassion. This mindset encourages individuals to treat themselves with kindness, acknowledge their common human experiences, and approach their own struggles with a balanced and non-judgmental perspective.

Swim like a duck in the journey of your life.

The phrase "swimming like a duck" is frequently used by people to describe themselves. This is a reference to how peaceful ducks appear above the water, yet how quickly they paddle beneath to keep afloat. Ducks take care of themselves and preen themselves so that when water touches their feathers, it easily rolls off.

How wonderful would it be for us humans to discover how to practice self-care in such a way that as pressures hit us daily, we too can let them 'roll off' our backs? This can be possible for humans by developing a self-compassionate mindset.

Source of image: Internet

26. Extend Self-compassion toward yourself, when?

Compassion can be directed towards oneself when suffering occurs without one's fault - when one's life's circumstances are just unpleasant or challenging to tolerate. However, when suffering is a result of one's own poor decisions, mistakes, or personality shortcomings, then also self-compassion is needed. Let us take an analogy from nature. There is a warning of a devastating cyclone. Your house is dismantled due to the force of the wind. This suffering was caused by an external agent. It was not your fault. Another example is, despite the warning of the cyclone you have entered sea waters. Your boat overturned and you are injured. You are injured because of your own mistake. You also require healing.

Let us take the example of two situations.

Example 1: You have a passion for flying. You decided to join the Air Force. You cleared the entrance test and interview also. But something happened, you got injured during the medical test, and you reached the hospital. Just unfortunate. You have to console yourself, maybe something better is waiting for you, and you opt for another career. This is a classic example of one's life's external conditions resulting in suffering and self-compassion needs to be extended towards oneself.

Example 2: There are times when our choices are wrong. You have limited time to prepare for the examination and you are partying. What will be the result? Either you will fail or perform poorly.

Here is another case. You have joined B.Tech . in mechanical engineering. After studying for one year, you start realizing, this is not your cup of tea. What can you do? Either drag yourself with the course and work in the field you have no passion for, or console yourself that you are leaving the course and wasting one year of life for a better life and better future in the field of your choice. This will be a better option. Here failure is because of your wrong preference and insufficient inquiry regarding the course you have joined. You also need self-compassion to correct yourself.

According to research, psychological well-being has a strong connection with self-compassion. Higher levels of self-compassion are associated with greater feelings of happiness, optimism, curiosity, and connectedness as well as an overall decrease in depression, anxiety, and failure-related fear. Self-compassionate people do not berate themselves when they fail; instead, they are more able to recognize, and admit mistakes, correct themselves, and change unproductive habits.

27. Master Tips and Tools to Grow in Life

Key to a better life

An anecdote from the reservoir of my childhood memories shall bring about the importance, essence, and relevance of what we mean by real growth.

During every summer vacation, we used to go to my grandfather's place in Dehradun to celebrate my birthday and also to get precious pearls of wisdom as a birthday present that have stayed with me ever since. Like every year, on my seventh birthday I was looking forward to learning something new. However, to my surprise, my grandfather gifted me a sapling and asked me to plant it in the backyard.

Initially, lots of care is needed after planting a sapling. We have to water the plant, give manure, and protect the plant from extreme weather. Gradually it grows fully.

After fifteen years when I visited my grandfather's house that sapling had grown into a huge tree, full of fruits, enriching the environment by supplying oxygen, becoming a shelter for several birds, and a constant supplier of life-giving gases.

Its existence is not for itself alone but for others too. That is real growth.

Change is the law of nature. Life becomes static without growth. Growth and personal life changes are not always very pleasant experiences. To gain something we have to lose something like indulging in unproductive or even negative patterns like spending too much time in pleasure-giving activities. To climb the ladder of life, you have to sweat and work hard.

Carl Rogers, one of the fathers of humanistic psychology, observed that people who made progress in their lives are not very content with their present status. He writes: "The good life is a process, not a state of being' (1961: 186) Life is not a bed of roses for them. They grow in their personal life by passing many difficult tests, changes, and losses."

Tips and Tools Used by Those Who Grow in Life

Personal development workout

Those who do well in life have a vision of growth before them. To clarify the direction of life they imagine their life 10-20 years ahead. What kind of person they would be, leading what kind of life? Accordingly, they equip themselves with the required skills for the future.

Water collected in one place stagnates, and so is life. Without progress, life loses its charm. With the growth in life comes happiness. "Strength and growth come only through continuous effort and struggle." – Oliver Napoleon Hill.

Everyone loves to be on top of the mountain. You have to climb the mountain for that pleasure!

Be Committed to Challenges in Life: Commitment to challenges in life is about drawing satisfaction and fulfillment from something that enhances your capability and enhances growth. They enjoy challenges that stretch their abilities.

Valuing Delayed Gratification:

The "Stanford Marshmallow Experiment", one of the most well-known psychology research projects, illustrates the importance of delayed gratification. Preschool students were given the option of eating a marshmallow right away or waiting fifteen minutes and receiving two marshmallows in Walter Mischel's 1972 experiment.

According to the longitudinal research, those who were able

to resist temptation proved more competent as adolescents and also performed academically better in later years of life. (Shoda et al., 1990).

Grit, or the Capacity to Sustain Effort:

Recently, it was discovered that the ability to sustain effort and persevere in the face of challenges is more significant than IQ in predicting academic achievement and long-term success. Those who want to grow in life do not leave things to fate. Their ceaseless sustained efforts to achieve the desired goal of their life give them success in life. They are not afraid of failure.

"Grit is a key factor in exceptional achievement. Grit is passion and perseverance for very long-term goals." —Angela Duckworth

Angela Duckworth wanted to know why some people achieve more than others. The importance of intelligence was something she was aware of. Even while intelligence is one of the best predictors of success, its effects are not powerful enough to fully explain why some people are able to do great things while others are not. The concept of grit developed as a result of her research. "Grit is passion and perseverance for very long-term goals. It is a strong predictor of success that is relatively independent of intelligence."

Duckworth and colleagues defined two major factors that are characteristic of gritty individuals:

- **Perseverance**: Exceptional sustained effort toward achieving a long-term goal.
- **Passion**: Commitment to consistent long-term goals over time.

"Grit entails working strenuously toward challenges, maintaining effort and interest over years despite failure, adversity, and plateaus in progress. The gritty individual approaches achievement as a marathon; his or her advantage is stamina."— Angela Duckworth, Journal of Personality and Social Psychology

Transcending Oneself for the Sake of the Greater Good.

Dedication and devotion to something or someone other than oneself are associated with transcendence. Finding one's life's purpose and living according to it are the key components. To achieve this goal, one must, however, go beyond the personal (without losing who they are) for the sake of something more than themselves. This something greater than themselves can be children, community service, meaningful work, helping the needy, or a spiritual path. Transcendence leads to virtuous living. For example, a highly qualified mother leaves her job because her children want her attention. Another example is a famous doctor who devotes one full day to serving the poor and needy in remote areas and giving medical advice and medicines without charging anything.

Transcendence is a eudemonic pathway to well-being. It can co-exist with personal growth. While growing, one can always spare some time, or resources for the welfare of others. Our culture emphasizes so much on 'Paropkar'(charity).

What is the difference between good humans and base /ignoble humans?

Good humans do not live for themselves alone. They live for the betterment of others also. One can be satisfied with one's life if one wants to pursue happiness and succeeds in doing so, or if one decides to live a more eudemonic-focused existence and succeeds in doing so. Eudemonic is pursuing happiness by finding meaning and purpose in life.

According to Diener, life satisfaction is nothing more than a congruence between the present and an ideal state, both of which are reflections of the individual's subjective evaluation of life. As a result, life satisfaction can be defined as an independent, subjective evaluation of one's current life situation, which can be hedonic (relating to, or characterized by pleasure) or eudemonic oriented (refers to striving to do what is meaningful). Eudaimonia, or happiness, combined with moral virtue, is the key to a better life and society.

28. The Yin and Yang of Self-Compassion

"Compassion is aimed at the alleviation of suffering – that of others or ourselves – and can be ferocious as well as tender" Kristin Neff.

The yin and yang concept, often depicted as yin-yang, is a fundamental Chinese philosophy that proposes the existence of opposing yet intertwined forces that interact to influence human well-being and life. It is portrayed as a circular black-and-white symbol. (Cherry,2023)

The Yin and Yang of compassion involve both the gentle and fierce sides, creating a balance in how we care for others and ourselves. Let's break it down with examples:

The Gentle Yin of Compassion:

This represents the soft, nurturing, and understanding aspect of compassion. It's about showing kindness and empathy, even when someone is going through a tough time. For example, if your friend is feeling down because he failed an important test, the gentle side of compassion would involve listening to him without judgment, offering a shoulder to cry on, and reassuring him that it's okay to make mistakes.

The Fierce Yang of Compassion:

This represents the more assertive and protective aspect of compassion. It's about taking action, when necessary, even if it means being firm to protect someone's well-being. For instance, if you see someone being bullied at school or work, the fierce side of compassion would involve speaking up and taking a stand against the bully, even if it means confronting rowdy people or seeking help from authorities to ensure the victim's safety.

So, the Yin and Yang of compassion is all about finding the balance between being gentle and empathetic when someone needs emotional support and being fierce and proactive when someone's well-being or rights are at stake. This balance ensures that we can care for others in a way that respects their emotions and boundaries while also advocating for their best interests and safety when required.

Source of image: Internet

Part Four

Navigating Life's Challenges: The Path to Worldly Wisdom

29. Time Management: What & When

"A plan is what, a schedule is when. It takes both a plan and a schedule to get things done." -Peter Turla

In a class of 30 students, 2 students are at the top of the ladder. The rest of the students are not able to manage that well. All are in the same class, have the same resources, the same team of teachers but the result is different. The same is the case for professionals. Two persons join the company with the same qualifications, one becomes the CEO of the company, but the other could not do that well.

You can be surrounded by individuals who manage to complete everything on their agenda. How do they manage to do so much in such a short period? The answer is their skill of time management. Time management is the process of organizing and allocating time between tasks, to maximize productivity and achieve goals.

Advantages of Effective Time Management:

- decreases stress

- improves work performance and life enjoyment.

Successful individuals are not born to be productive. Rather, they are learning and practicing the skills that are necessary to accomplish more in less time. Productivity is not a talent. This is a learning skill that each individual must learn and develop.

Planning Time Management Journey

"The bad news is time flies. The good news is you're the pilot" - Michael Altshuler

Beginning your time management journey with a strategy establishes a solid basis for future habits, boosting your chances of success.

Be Realistic About How Much You Can Accomplish in the Given Time

First and foremost, determine actually where you are spending your time. There is frequently a mismatch between what we believe is taking time and actually what it is. This is due to people's misunderstanding of how long a task takes. Assume you need to send a 300-word email. "It's simple to compose an email. It should take no longer than five minutes." However, you overestimate your speed while underestimating all the small, relevant activities that must be completed to attain your final goal. Maybe evaluating, proofreading, language selection, and locating email addresses can all add time to your tasks. With these modifications, a 5-minute email took 20 minutes!

Assume you have the same issue with some jobs on your list. What begins as a balanced task is almost always transformed into a hectic to-do list as the day progresses. You must be realistic about what you are capable of accomplishing and how you spend your time. As a result, constructing a time balance sheet is beneficial.

Keep track of everything you do to gain a clear picture of how you use your time.

Examine your report at the end of the week and evaluate the time spent on various chores. With this information, you can readily identify areas that need improvement. For example, you could be wasting time sitting in unproductive meetings or doing a lot of work. With this information, you can understand how you spend your time and plan accordingly. This brings us to the next step which is 4ds of the time management.

4Ds of the Time Management

Establish realistic objectives and arrange your tasks in order of importance. If your workload appears overwhelming, even with effective time management, consider employing the 4Ds of Time Management: Delete, Delegate, Defer, and Do. This approach categorizes tasks into four distinct groups, aiding in task prioritization.

Delete

"Deciding what not to do is as important as deciding what to do." – Steve Jobs

Delete and "Drop" both refer to the idea of eliminating pointless and unessential items from your to-do list. The first step is to let go of any pointless and trivial professional and personal obligations.

Analyse your everyday activities and pinpoint the top-time thieves. Get rid of them.

- If you are the head of the organization with multiple responsibilities, avoid attending meetings that aren't required or relevant to your job. Reduce the time to be spent in meetings.

- Emails: Maintain a tidy inbox. Sometimes you are inundated with spam or commercial emails, which is a time- and energy-consuming waste. You should unsubscribe from those emails.

- Say No: Be able to decline tasks when someone makes an unanticipated request, or complete them as quickly as you can. Before committing to extra tasks to your list, go over your current to-do list.

Delegate

If you have work that needs to be done but will take up too much of your time, you should assign it to someone else. A delegate is someone who manages a task or project on your behalf.

One person cannot do all the work in an organization. Consider a scenario where you're overseeing a marketing project that requires extensive data analysis and report generation. While you might possess the skills to conduct the analysis, your expertise in strategy development and client communication could be better utilized in handling critical client meetings. In this case, delegating the data analysis to a competent analyst within your team allows you to focus on high-level strategic planning and client management, ensuring a more efficient and balanced workflow.

Defer

"People who can focus get things done. People who can prioritize get the right things done." – John Maeda

Defer is another name for delay, which is a technique for putting off tasks that don't require immediate attention. When you have the time or are free, you can schedule it. Deferring means saying no to tasks of lower priority. The main idea behind the 'defer concept' is that if you can't eliminate some tasks from your to-do list but don't feel like spending time on them presently, you can delay them for later. For instance, going to the movies with friends is not necessary right now, you may schedule it for weekends. If you get an email, don't worry about reading it and answering right away. Because not all emails require immediate response, schedule a time to respond and check your inbox.

Do

Do represents the final and fourth Ds of time management. "Do" refers to any tasks that need to be done as soon as possible, usually within a few minutes. These urgent tasks come after filtering tasks through the previous 3D steps.

These kinds of tasks are typically critical and time-sensitive. The penalties of not performing them could ruin your life or profession, thus it needs to be accomplished as soon as possible. Avoid piling up these tasks; instead, finish them as soon as you can like submitting your admission or job application before the last date.

These are a few examples of "do" tasks:

Urgent tasks: Urgent tasks to be completed in a set time frame: that must be completed immediately like submitting a project, printing a report, sending a letter, answering an important call, attending to urgent issues, etc.

Scheduled tasks: A scheduled task is something you have been given to complete by the deadline. Scheduled tasks include things like going to meetings, making presentations, and working on projects, tasks assigned to you by your superior, etc.

Two-minute tasks: If the task can be finished in under two minutes and will help your career or your life, you should do it right away.

These methods help you determine which tasks should be prioritized, and which tasks should be planned and scheduled, delegated, or eliminated. Whatever your goals are, they should be SMART: specific, measurable, achievable, relevant, and timely.

Start Week with a Strategy

Plan your week on Sunday. Starting the week with a strategy allows you to focus on your top priorities. It also helps with the transition from a relaxed weekend mindset to a productive Monday morning "work brain." Spend a few minutes on Sunday planning your week. Break down your weekly goals into daily chores to increase your chances of accomplishment. So, you can know what you need to do each day at a glance.

Take advantage of the golden hour or biological prime time.

Do you know what time of day you work best? Knowing this can assist you in optimizing your workload. Divide your day between 3-5 parts to identify your golden hour or biological prime time. Track your productivity for the week in your notebook or using a free time monitoring application. Rank these hours from most productive to least productive after the week. Once you've discovered the golden hour, you may schedule your week appropriately. **Schedule difficult or complex chores during productive hours/periods.**

Meet Emily

Let's delve into an academic scenario to illustrate the importance of starting the week with a strategic approach. Meet Emily, a diligent college student with a passion for astrophysics. Emily believes in the power of planning and how it can transform her academic journey. Every Sunday, she sits down with her favourite cup of coffee and maps out her week. She breaks down her overarching goals, like mastering quantum mechanics or acing her upcoming astrophysics exam into daily tasks, which might include reading specific chapters, practicing problem sets, and reviewing her notes.

Emily understands her own natural rhythms and the value of her "golden hour." Through meticulous tracking in her trusty astrophysics-themed notebook, she pinpoints that her mind sparkles the brightest between 9 a.m. and 11 a.m. During these hours, she tackles the most complex theories and calculations with ease, leveraging her peak mental acuity. She uses her smartphone's time-tracking app to monitor her productivity levels throughout the week, noting her high-energy and low-energy periods.

Besides her to-do list, Emily includes a "stellar achievements" list, where she highlights unexpected academic victories. For instance, understanding a particularly complex concept or solving a challenging problem earns a special spot on this list. Every Sunday, she celebrates these wins, boosting her confidence and reinforcing her commitment to academic excellence.

Recognizing the perils of procrastination, Emily resolves to start her day early. She knows that advanced planning not only prevents last-minute panic but also allows her to handle any cosmic disruptions that may arise, such as unexpected power failure or internet glitches. By submitting her assignments, a day before the deadline, Emily ensures that she always has a cushion for any unforeseen circumstances.

With her astute time management skills and preparedness for the unknown, Emily confidently navigates the vast universe of academia, equipped with the tools to excel in her studies and reach for the stars.

Include a "done list" beside your to-do list. Unexpected tasks will come during the day, regardless of how well you prepare. Write them down on a separate list next to your to-dos for more satisfaction at the end of the day. Consider your accomplishments from the previous week and celebrate them on Sunday. This evaluation period will boost your confidence while also supporting you in making plans for the future week.

Start your day early.

Many people believe that they perform best under extreme deadline pressure, therefore they put off doing their work until the day before the deadline. This, however, is not always the case. Projects frequently take longer than intended, making completion challenging. Push the deadline and meet it. **Always aim to submit your work one day in advance**.

Your time management should also cater for sudden unavoidable natural and man-made emergencies like power cuts, emergencies, shortages of essential items, etc.

Make your time management system a habit.

The aforementioned concepts must be developed into lasting routines. You may cultivate a more productive mindset by continuing to put these time management strategies into practice. Make a sensible timetable that you can stick to for a long time—at least a month. Over time, these processes will become increasingly automated.

"Life isn't about waiting for the time to come. It's all about making the most of things in the time that is given to you."— Joel Brown

Source of image: Internet

30. Learn to Adjust and Adapt

Change is the law of nature. As we grow, we move also. One of my friends joined the hostel because the place where her father was posted did not have good schools. Naturally, she has to be away from her family for her studies. She could not adjust to the hostel environment. She became homesick. She was not able to concentrate on her studies. That resulted in bad grades. As the shadows of fear and concern began to cast a shadow over her mind, she started getting panic attacks. This is a classic example of someone who finds it difficult to cope with change.

Life is full of stress.

Coping usually involves responding positively to or tolerating unfavourable events or circumstances while maintaining a positive self-image and emotional balance. Coping takes place in the context of perceived stressful life changes. In the case of the above-mentioned student, for her hostel life was stressful because it was a changed environment where she was required to be independent and self-caring. The comfort zone of the family suddenly disappeared for the girl.

Let us take the example of Sarah, a bright and ambitious student who embarked on her college journey far away from her hometown. Her first few weeks in the hostel were filled with excitement and the thrill of newfound independence. However, as the academic pressure intensified and the challenges of living away from home started to take a toll, Sarah found herself struggling to cope.

With mounting coursework and a sense of homesickness creeping in, Sarah initially felt overwhelmed. She missed the comfort of her family's support and the familiarity of her home environment. Yet, determined to overcome these hurdles, she began to explore various coping strategies.

To combat her homesickness, Sarah made an effort to connect with her hostel mates, participating in group activities and forming study groups. These newfound friendships provided her with a strong support network, allowing her to share her concerns and seek guidance from peers who were experiencing similar challenges.

Recognizing the importance of maintaining a balanced lifestyle, Sarah dedicated time to pursue her hobbies and engage in recreational activities. Regular yoga sessions and evening walks around the hostel campus helped her to relax and unwind, reducing her stress levels and improving her overall well-being.

As her coursework became more demanding, Sarah learned to manage her time efficiently. She created a study schedule that allowed her to stay organized and focused on her academic goals. With the support of her hostel warden, she sought additional academic guidance and resources, enabling her to enhance her understanding of complex subjects and excel in her studies.

Despite the initial struggles, Sarah's resilience and determination allowed her to thrive in the hostel environment. Through building meaningful connections, prioritizing self-care, and adopting effective time management techniques, she not only coped with the challenges but also flourished in her academic and personal endeavours, creating lasting memories and friendships that would stay with her long after her hostel days.

Coping involves adapting to unexpected demands or pressures. This necessitates a bigger effort and use of energy than is required in normal life tasks. Adopting a coping mechanism will help here. Some common coping mechanisms are lowering expectations, keeping emotionally helpful connections, maintaining emotional serenity, or expressing painful emotions are some examples of popular coping methods. Challenge any beliefs you once held that are no longer helpful. Make a direct effort to alter the source of stress, keep your distance from the stressor, and request assistance or help from others.

31. Motivation

Inculcate Goal Oriented Behaviour

What is motivation?

The word motivation is coined from the Latin word "movere", which means to move. Famous players and researchers are all highly motivated people. Were they born like this? Did the nurse in the maternity ward hand over the baby to the parents, saying, 'Hold the researcher'? No. Such people are highly motivated people. They had a drive in them. They had a strong desire to do something. **Motivation is an internal drive that activates behaviour and gives it direction.**

Consider the life of Marie Curie, a prominent physicist and chemist renowned for her groundbreaking research on radioactivity. Curie, born in 1867 in Poland, demonstrated exceptional intrinsic motivation and a relentless pursuit of scientific knowledge from an early age. Despite facing numerous obstacles, including gender discrimination in the field of science, she remained resolute in her quest for discovery.

Driven by her innate passion for understanding the fundamental properties of matter, Curie delved into the study of radioactivity, ultimately leading to her discovery of two new elements, polonium and radium. Her unwavering dedication to her research and her commitment to advancing the field of science earned her two Nobel Prizes, one in Physics and another in Chemistry, making her the first woman to receive such honors.

Curie's tenacity and unyielding spirit not only revolutionized the field of physics and chemistry but also paved the way for future generations of scientists. Her profound legacy serves as a testament to the transformative power of intrinsic motivation, underscoring the notion that genuine passion and an unwavering commitment to knowledge can shape the course of history and inspire countless others to pursue their own intellectual endeavor.

Motivation is the activation of goal-oriented behaviour. Motivation is said to be intrinsic or extrinsic.

Intrinsically Motivated v/s Extrinsically Motivated

You must be having a pet dog. When you want to train your dog, you give a bone or a biscuit as reward for his desired behaviour like shaking hand, catching objects or fetching a ball.

Research has revealed that individuals who are intrinsically motivated to learn, do so for the pleasure of learning, rather than for external rewards while those who are extrinsically motivated to learn, are motivated to learn for the external rewards that learning will bring. The dog in the above example was extrinsically motivated to learn. The desired behaviour of shaking hands, and fetching the ball was the result of the biscuit and the bone that was motivating him.

Intrinsic Motivation Leads to Academic and Professional Success

The students with high academic motivation, who are intrinsically motivated are more likely to have increased levels of academic achievement and have lower dropout rates. This has been observed that achievement-motivated people evidenced a significantly higher rate of advancement in their company compared to others in the world of work. It is therefore recommended that parents and teachers should endeavor to promote and encourage academic motivation in students from an early age seeing the importance it plays in forming self-concepts, values, and beliefs that students hold about themselves.

Drive to Go On

The drive to achieve one's goals is among the most vital factors in the life of a person. Alen Musk and Mahender Singh Dhoni are two examples of individuals who stand out from the crowd. They are driven. Motivation is the term used to describe this drive in every facet of one's life—student life, career, personal, or professional—it is a zeal and determination accompanied by a certain zest that motivates one to persevere and accomplish greater heights.

The drive to go on, a central tenet of worldly wisdom, encapsulates the resilience and inner strength that enable individuals to persevere through life's most daunting challenges. It represents the unwavering determination to continue forward, despite obstacles and adversities, in pursuit of personal growth and fulfillment. This intrinsic motivation, deeply rooted in the human spirit, often emerges in moments of crisis or profound personal struggle, shaping individuals into beacons of hope and inspiration for those around them.

One example of the unyielding drive to go on is the remarkable story of Malala Yousafzai, a Pakistani activist for female education and the youngest Nobel Prize laureate. Malala's unwavering commitment to education and gender equality became evident at a young age, as she bravely defied the Taliban's oppressive regime, advocating for the rights of girls to receive education. Despite facing grave threats to her life, Malala remained resolute in her mission, driven by an unwavering belief in the transformative power of education.

Her courage and determination led to a fateful assassination attempt by the Taliban in 2012, resulting in life-threatening injuries. However, even in the face of this unspeakable violence, Malala's spirit remained unbroken. Her resilience and determination to recover and continue her mission served as a symbol of hope and resilience for millions around the world.

Malala's unwavering drive to go on, to stand up for what she believed in, and to fight for the rights of all children to receive an education, transcended her personal struggles and inspired a global movement. Her remarkable journey underscores the transformative power of perseverance and the profound impact that one individual's determination can have on the world. Through her story, the drive to go on emerges as a testament to the indomitable human spirit and a catalyst for positive change in the face of adversity.

From where does the drive come?

The drive could be internal or external in origin. This is decided by the person. You have the ambition and motivation to work hard to achieve your goal of becoming a doctor so that you can serve humanity. You will develop the abilities necessary to help you.

As one moves up the ladder of maturity and age, the things that motivate them change. Additionally, achieving one goal initiates the process of achieving another. Being motivated is thus always needed. There are times when one experiences a demotivating phase, feels down, and everything appears hopeless. Then, they must determine what would motivate them back into action: reading inspirational books, conversing with people who are always inspired, or spending time in nature. Every person has a unique driving force at work. You must recognize what motivates you.

Need to occasionally take a stalk

Some people periodically reevaluate their objectives and aspirations in order to motivate themselves to accomplish greater tasks with newer degrees of excitement. Every now and then, one needs to take a look around to get the inspiration they need to keep going.

Intrinsically motivated students and professionals are

Successful in life.

In conclusion, for students, the exploration of intrinsic motivation illuminates a crucial pathway to academic success and personal growth. By nurturing a genuine passion for learning and embracing the inherent joy of knowledge acquisition, students can unlock their full potential and pave the way for a fulfilling educational journey. Leveraging intrinsic motivation as a driving force not only enhances academic performance but also fosters a resilient mindset, empowering students to navigate the challenges of learning with confidence and perseverance. By cultivating a deep-seated love for their chosen fields of study, students can embark on a transformative learning experience, one that paves the way for a lifelong commitment to curiosity, creativity, and personal excellence.

In the realm of professional endeavours, the significance of intrinsic motivation becomes ever more apparent, serving as a cornerstone for exceptional performance and career satisfaction. By harnessing their innate passion for their work and aligning their professional goals with personal values, professionals can foster a thriving work environment characterized by creativity, innovation, and resilience. Embracing intrinsic motivation as a guiding principle not only propels individuals toward professional success but also nurtures a profound sense of purpose and fulfilment in their chosen careers. Through the cultivation of intrinsic drivers, professionals can navigate the complexities of the modern workplace with unwavering determination, fostering a culture of excellence and contributing to a dynamic, fulfilling, and impactful professional journey.

32. Overcoming Obsession

Don't let the obsession devastate you.

Obsession can both balance and unbalance us. Timely obsession with something can make our life. Untimely obsession harms us and deviates us from our goals. Obsession with your ex-boyfriend or girlfriend, who has ended the relationship is going to harm you. You have to be practical in life. You can't live in the dream world of obsession. You have to learn to come out of that emotional world. You need to develop the ability to leave that emotional realm.

William was an emotional boy. He became very pally with his childhood friend Anni. Both studied in the same school and later joined different colleges for professional courses. Both remained in touch during college education also. Anni was ambitious. By nature, she was caring. William thought of her closeness as love for him. When he settled in life, he proposed to her. Anni got the shock of her life. She explained to William, that they were just friends and nothing more. They have to move in different directions. For her, the friendship ended. But William was obsessed. He continued frequently visiting places, where he thought Anni might come. Lost in his one-sided love, he became unbalanced and became depressed.

Obsession can throw us off balance

Obsession sometimes throws us off balance, just like other addictions do. There are many aspects of our lives that we start to neglect. If obsession becomes overly consumed, it lets us accept the decline and even breakdown of important aspects of our lives. But, even if our lives are still in balance if the object of our obsession is taken away from us, as in the case of William, we find ourselves heartbroken and frequently feel as though we have lost all hope of ever finding happiness.

Positivity of obsession: Obsession is not always devastating. If we are obsessed with something at the right time and place, it can be a boon. In fact, the extra energy, motivation, determination, and strength that obsession brings can be really useful if we use it in the right way. Furthermore, we must accept that achieving greatness without a modicum of obsession is difficult. When used to our advantage, obsession may bring out the best in us, inspiring us to use our creativity and intellect to find solutions to extremely challenging issues. In other words, obsession can help us achieve greatness if rightly placed. Recently researchers developed the vaccine for coronavirus. It was the obsession to overcome the challenge of the virus that drove the researchers to find a vaccine that saved millions of lives. On the other hand, an obsession to develop a virus to use as a biological weapon is devastating.

"Determination becomes an obsession and then it becomes all that matters." - Jeremy Irvine

When you are aiming for an outstanding existence, obsession is necessary. To avoid becoming a wage slave who lives only to pay their bills like the majority, you must become obsessed with the grind. I hope this chapter will inspire you to believe in your dream and to be obsessed with your ambition to turn it into reality. Let your obsession function positively. Allow your obsession to serve you positively.

Source of image: Internet

33. Avoid Toxic Persons

The term "toxic" is used to characterize a wide range of environmental, social, and health problems. This buzzword, which refers to everything from toxic waste to toxic workplaces, was selected as Oxford Dictionaries Word of the Year in 2018.

You must have heard about toxic environments, there are toxic people too, who spread negativity. Does someone in your life frequently make you feel confused, irritated, frustrated, or guilty? If so, you may be conversing with a toxic individual. Persons with toxic traits may behave in a way that's hurtful and damaging to those around them. Their actions, words, and energy might affect others negatively — whether they realize it or not. At some point in your life, you may encounter a person with these types of traits. Maybe it's a co-worker, partner, sibling, or even a parent.

Traits of a Toxic Person

Identifying the traits of a toxic person can be crucial in protecting your well-being and maintaining healthy relationships. Here are some common traits of toxic individuals:

Constant Criticism: Toxic individuals often habitually criticize and belittle others, focusing on their flaws rather than their strengths.

Manipulative Behaviour: They may use manipulation tactics to control or influence others for their own benefit, often without considering the well-being of those around them.

Lack of Empathy: They may show little or no empathy for others' feelings or experiences, disregarding the impact of their words or actions on those around

Insecurity: Toxic individuals may exhibit signs of deep insecurity, leading them to project their negative feelings onto others and engage in behaviours that elevate their own self-esteem at the expense of others.

Constant Drama: They tend to create or thrive on drama and conflict, often stirring up trouble or engaging in gossip to maintain a sense of control or power within their social circle.

Jealousy and Envy: They may express intense jealousy or envy toward the success or happiness of others, often trying to undermine or sabotage their achievements.

Lack of Accountability: Toxic individuals often refuse to take responsibility for their actions, deflecting blame onto others or external circumstances, and may not apologize or make amends for their harmful behaviour.

Negativity: They tend to have a consistently negative outlook on life, frequently focusing on the worst possible outcomes and draining the energy and optimism of those around them.

Boundary Violation: They may disrespect personal boundaries, often crossing lines without regard for others' comfort or consent, whether it's physical, emotional, or psychological boundaries.

Controlling Behaviour: Toxic individuals may exhibit controlling behaviour, attempting to dictate the actions and decisions of others, and becoming agitated when they do not get their way.

Recognizing these traits can help you establish healthier boundaries and navigate interactions with toxic individuals more effectively. It is crucial to prioritize your emotional well-being and seek support from trusted friends or professionals when dealing with such individuals.

Managing a toxic individual in a school or college
Managing a toxic individual in a school or college environment can be particularly challenging, as students often have limited control over their surroundings. Here's a guide on how to manage toxic behaviour from a peer in a school or college setting:

Set Personal Boundaries: Clearly define what is acceptable and what is not. Avoid engaging in activities or discussions that compromise your values or well-being. If necessary, communicate your boundaries directly to the toxic individual in a calm and assertive manner.

Limit Interaction: Minimize interactions with the toxic person as much as possible. This might involve avoiding spending unnecessary time with them and limiting your communication to essential or academic matters only.

Seek Support from Friends and Teachers: Share your concerns with friends or trustworthy peers who can offer emotional support and guidance. Additionally, consider discussing the situation with a trusted teacher, counsellor, or school advisor who can provide advice and assistance in managing the issue.

Stay Calm and Composed: If the toxic person attempts to

provoke you, try your best to remain calm and composed. Responding to their behaviour with aggression or retaliation might escalate the situation and create further tension.

Engage in Positive Activities: Surround yourself with positive and like-minded individuals who share your interests and values. Participate in extracurricular activities, clubs, or groups that promote a healthy and supportive social environment.

Document Incidents: Keep a record of any instances of toxic behaviour that significantly affect your well-being or academic performance. This documentation can serve as evidence if you decide to report the issue to a teacher, school counsellor, or principal.

Seek Mediation or Intervention: If the situation persists or escalates, consider requesting the assistance of a school counsellor, teacher, or an appropriate authority figure to mediate the conflict and find a resolution.

Focus on Personal Development: Concentrate on your personal growth, academic success, and overall well-being. Allocate time for self-care activities, hobbies, and interests that promote a positive and fulfilling school experience.

Remember that managing a toxic person in a school or college setting requires patience and resilience. It is essential to prioritize your emotional well-being and seek the necessary support from trusted peers and school authorities when needed.

Source of image: Internet

34. Managing Anger
Control Your Temper

"For every minute you remain angry, you give up sixty seconds of peace of mind." – Ralph Waldo Emerson

Once upon a time, there was a boy who had a very bad temper. His father gave him a bag of nails and told him that every time the boy lost his temper, he had to hammer a nail into the fence. The boy hammered 37 nails into the fence on the first day. Over the next few weeks, the boy gradually learned to control his temper, and the number of nails he hammered into the fence decreased. He discovered that controlling his temper was easier than hammering those nails into the fence.

Finally, a day came when the boy did not lose his cool. He told his father the news, and his father suggested that the boy pull out a nail every day to keep his temper under control. After a few days, the young boy was finally able to tell his father that all of the nails had been removed. The father led his son to the fence by the hand. He said, "You did well, my son, but look at the holes in the fence. The fence will never be the same again. When you say things in anger, they leave scars like this one."

Moral of the story: Control your anger, and don't say things to people in the heat of the moment, that you may later regret. Some things in life, you are unable to take back.

"The man who gives way to anger, or hatred, or any other passion, cannot work; he only breaks himself to pieces, and does nothing practical. It is the calm, forgiving, equable, well-balanced mind that does the greatest amount of work." - Swami Vivekananda

Anger can destroy the foundation of who we are

Anger can destroy the foundation of who we are, hijacking our emotions and our capacity for reason and, as the Stoic philosopher Epictetus teaches us, drags us down to the level of a wild beast, petty and malignant.

Anger is a negative thought

"Anger, if not restrained, is frequently more hurtful to us than the injury that provokes it."

- Seneca the Younger

Anger is a negative thought, it is an emotion that tears apart the foundation of who we are by leading us to act in ways that are inconsistent with our values, morals, and beliefs. This causes us to drift farther and farther from the person we want to be and the life we want to lead. This pressure frequently leads to immoral, harmful, and unvirtuous behaviour. Anger is temporary insanity. We should never act with insanity.

Anger is not always bad according to Aristotle. If we are angry for the right reason at the right place, it can be beneficial also. People have done great inventions in anger.

One contemporary example that illustrates the constructive use of anger is the movement for climate action led by young activist Greta Thunberg. Driven by her frustration and anger at the lack of sufficient action to address the global climate crisis, she initiated the "Fridays for Future" movement. Through her passionate speeches and activism, she has brought global attention to the urgency of addressing climate change.

Her anger at the inaction of political leaders and policymakers has mobilized millions of people worldwide to join the movement for climate justice, leading to increased awareness, policy changes, and commitments to sustainable practices. Greta Thunberg's impactful advocacy demonstrates how channeling anger into productive action can bring about significant positive changes for the benefit of the planet and future generations.

How to Control Anger

"The reason why we have two ears and only one mouth is that we may listen the more and talk the less." — Zeno

Find the root cause of anger: Analyse what triggered your anger and make an advance decision on how to handle the situation. What makes you angry? Try to get rid of that first.

Address anger timely: If anger is ignored for a prolonged period, it will spiral out of control. Unrest at work is an example of this. If labour dissatisfaction is not addressed promptly, it may flare up.

Avoid spending time with irritating and aggressive people: Moods are contagious. Avoid spending time with irritable and aggressive people. The company of calm and pleasant people will be beneficial.

Our ability to be creative can help us relax: Fine arts and music do not make us angry. An angry mood cannot exist in a serene mind. Take up whatever hobby soothes your temper, or learn to play an instrument.

Manipulate the environment: Instead of environments that irritate you, seek out ones that are attractive to the eye. Look for settings with pleasing hues. Our moods may be impacted by environmental influences.

Avoid Arguments: Try to avoid arguments when you're angry, sleepy, tired, or hungry as you'll be more prone to irritability, which can quickly turn into fury.

Self-deprecating Humour Helps: Self-deprecating humour refers to the act of making oneself the butt of jokes or humorous remarks. While anger is often associated with a lack of humour, self-deprecating humour can actually help alleviate intense emotions, including anger, by providing a way to cope with difficult situations and emotions through laughter and self-awareness. This form of humour can help individuals gain perspective on their frustrations and potentially diffuse their anger by shifting their focus away from negative emotions. Here's an example to illustrate how self-deprecating humour can help in managing anger. Imagine a person, let's call him Sumit, who is working on an important project with a tight deadline. Due to some unforeseen technical issues, the project encounters a significant setback, which frustrates Sumit and triggers his anger. Instead of lashing out at his colleagues or venting his anger, Sumit decides to use self-deprecating humour to lighten the tension and diffuse his frustration. Sumit says, "Well, looks like my tech skills are so legendary that even the computer decided to take a day off when I'm around. Maybe I should switch to using a typewriter instead!"

By making this self-deprecating joke, Sumit acknowledges his own role in the setback while also injecting humour into the situation. This can help create a more light-hearted atmosphere, allowing both himself and his colleagues to see the situation from a different, less intense perspective. In this way, self-deprecating humour can act as a coping mechanism that allows individuals to acknowledge their own faults and imperfections while providing a release from intense emotions such as anger.

Try Postponing Tactics: Postpone your response. You can practice cognitive distance, or delaying your response, by going for a walk, using the restroom, or doing anything else that will take you away from the scenario.

Alter your physical state to alter your thoughts: Altering your physical state to manage anger involves making changes to your body's physical condition, such as your posture, breathing, or activity level, in order to influence your emotional and mental state. This approach is based on the idea that the mind and body are interconnected, and changes in one can affect the other. By consciously adjusting your physical state, you can often regulate and even shift your thoughts and emotions, including anger.

Here's an example to illustrate how altering your physical state can help manage anger.

Imagine a person, let's call her Sunita, who is experiencing a particularly frustrating day at work. A series of unexpected setbacks and conflicts have left her feeling extremely angry and overwhelmed. Sensing that her anger is escalating, Sunita decides to employ physical strategies to help manage her emotions.

She steps away from her desk, finds a quiet space, and focuses on her breathing. She takes deep, slow breaths, inhaling for a count of four, holding for a count of five, and exhaling for a count of six. This deliberate breathing technique helps her calm her racing heart and ease the tension in her body. Next, Sunita engages in a brief physical activity by taking a brisk walk around the office building. As she moves, she notices the physical sensations in her body, the breeze on her face, and the rhythm of her steps. This physical movement helps release some of the pent-up energy from her anger and allows her to gain a new perspective on her situation.

After a few minutes of mindful movement and controlled breathing, Sunita finds that her anger has diminished, and she is better able to approach the challenges of her day with a calmer and more rational mindset.

Never act in anger. These are some strategies to help you overcome anger.

Source of image: Internet

35. Seize the Opportunity or It Will Fly

Opportunity should be taken as soon as it knocks at your door because once it flies, it flies forever. Time does not turn back, so make the most of it to reap its rewards. The secret to success is seizing the opportunity that presents itself and not letting it slip.

The student's years in high school and college are the finest times to learn, comprehend, and acquire knowledge and wisdom. Although wisdom has no age restriction, one should continue to nurture it. During your time as a student, you must decide how your life will turn out. Taking advantage of the opportunity, understanding the value of hard work, and being consistent can help you advance and get to the right place in life.

The term "opportunity" finds its roots in Latin, signifying "towards the port." This linguistic history conjures the image of a ship skillfully using wind and tide to reach the safety of the harbour. Given life's fleeting nature, this serves as a strong incentive to make the most of the chances bestowed upon us by the divine.

An ancient Greek statue

An ancient Greek statue depicting a man with wings on his feet, a large lock of hair on the front of his head, and no hair at all on the back. Beneath is the inscription-

"What is thy name?

My name is Opportunity.

Why hast thou wing on thy feet?

That I may fly away swiftly.

Why hast thou a great forelock?

That man may seize me when I come.

Why art thou bald in the back?

That when I am gone by, none can lay hold of me."

Kairos: The God of Opportunity

Kairos is the Greek god of opportunity. Kairos, in Greek mythology, represents the concept of the "right" or "opportune" moment. Depicted as a young and fleeting deity, Kairos is often portrayed with wings on his feet, symbolizing the fleeting nature of opportunity. He is typically shown with a lock of hair on his forehead, but bald at the back, indicating that once the opportunity has passed, it cannot be grasped again.

The Romans also had a similar figure known as Ocasio, further emphasizing the idea of the fleeting nature of opportunities. Kairos embodies the idea that there are specific moments in life when action can lead to great success or positive outcomes, highlighting the importance of seizing these critical moments.

If you are in the secondary or senior secondary stage of education, this phase holds immense significance in shaping your future. Diverting your focus from rigorous studies to indulging in social media, parties, excessive phone usage, or constant messaging on platforms like WhatsApp can deter your concentration and hinder your academic performance. Failure to dedicate yourself to your studies during secondary school may result in missing out on the preferred academic stream, while in senior secondary education, it could impede admission to a desired professional course or prestigious university. This critical juncture significantly impacts your standing and the quality of your future life.

In life, there comes a moment when everyone seeks a change in fortunes, often manifested as an opportunity. We understand that opportunities are fleeting, delicate, and elusive. Therefore, it is imperative to recognize and seize them before they slip away.

"Time equals life; therefore, waste your time and waste your life, or master your time and master your life." This quote by Alan Lakein serves as a potent reminder of the swiftness of time. Failing to proactively set priorities and safeguard our time can lead to its squandering. Creating an "avoid at all costs list," distinguishing between the important and the urgent, and incorporating the word "no" into our vocabulary can help us manage our time more effectively.

Time is invaluable. It should not be allowed to slip through our fingers. Success comes to those who strive for it, who refrain from wasting time during their academic years, and who seize opportunities as they arise. Consider the case of Rajeev (name changed), a bright student who, six months before his exam, diverted his attention to subjects outside of the curriculum. As a consequence, he couldn't perform well in the exam and failed to secure admission to a good college. Being a capable person, he got good jobs later on but did not reach the position where he should have been.

Our tomorrow is chalked by what we are doing today. Those who work hard today will reap the benefits later in their life. It is very important to follow the correct track otherwise you will be lost. *"Your future is created by what you do today, not tomorrow."*- Douglas Adams

36. Learn to Say No

"You have to learn to say no without feeling guilty, setting boundaries is healthy. You need to learn to respect and take care of yourself. "Saying "no" comes more naturally to certain people than it does to others, who find it nearly impossible. Some people are very comfortable saying no when their plate is too full or they don't want to do something. There is another category of people who can't refuse, no matter how busy they are or how much they do not want to undertake work. They damage themselves because of this weakness.

One day, when I was meeting parents of students seeking admission to class XI. One young boy entered my office. Students are accompanied by their parents at the time of admission. As he came alone, the staff asked about his parents, he said he had come alone because his parents were not educated enough to fill his admission documents. He informed me that he topped the Bihar State Secondary Examination. When asked how would he pay the fee as his parents were not with him. Very confidently, he said, he had an ATM card. That was the time when only a few students were using Debit Cards for payment. Initially, he was working hard and doing well. But he was living in a boy's hostel away from his home. He became homesick. Other boys in the hostel coaxed him to try beer to feel better. Gradually he started smoking and taking drugs too. This energetic boy with a spark in his eyes changed into a drowsy person. He lost focus and failed.

Why did this happen? This happened because he did not know how to say no. He was alone and depressed. He could not say no to the peer pressure, that was pushing him towards a destructive path.

This same boy came to see me after three years and informed me that he cleared the entrance test of medical college and is pursuing an M.B.B.S. He realized his mistake and said no to wrong things not in his interest. This awakening came to him at the right time, and he attained the target he wanted to achieve.

"Let today mark a new beginning for you. Give yourself permission to say NO without feeling guilty, mean, or selfish, anybody who gets upset and/or expects you to say YES all of the time clearly doesn't have your best interest at heart, always remember: You have a right to say NO without having to explain yourself, Be at peace with your decisions." – Stephanie Lahart

All kinds of pressures come in life. We have to realize and learn to differentiate between right and wrong and carry forward in our journey of life.

37. Empower the Weak

Two young boys approached me. They introduced themselves as volunteers at an orphanage that rescues and takes care of children left in garbage bins. I thought like other volunteers they would expect some donation. Hence, I asked my P.A. to get my cheque book.

They immediately retorted, "We don't want any charity. We don't want anyone to pity these abandoned children. We are not looking for sympathy but empathy. We wish to sell handmade cards prepared by these children of the orphanage. This will not only instill confidence and self-esteem in children but also pave the way for them to be self-reliant and empowered".

The next day they appealed in the school assembly to the students to come forward for the noble cause and buy New Year greeting cards. They ended up selling 500 cards, earning a handsome amount!

A remarkable true story that embodies the spirit of empowerment is that of Wilma Rudolph, who overcame significant physical challenges to become an Olympic champion. Born prematurely in 1940, Wilma contracted polio at the age of five, which left her with a paralyzed leg. Despite facing considerable adversity, Wilma refused to be defined by her condition.

With the unwavering support of her family and through her own determination, Wilma underwent years of rigorous physical therapy and exercises. Slowly but steadily, she regained strength and mobility in her leg, eventually gaining the ability to walk without supports. Her resilience and perseverance were further fuelled by her love for running, and she began training and competing in various track and field events.

In the 1960 Rome Olympics, Wilma Rudolph defied all odds

and became the first American woman to win three gold medals in track and field during a single Olympic Games. Her remarkable achievements not only shattered records but also inspired generations of athletes and individuals around the world, proving that with dedication and perseverance, any obstacle can be conquered.

Wilma Rudolph's story is a testament to the power of inner strength and resilience. It serves as a powerful reminder that with determination and a refusal to be defined by circumstances, individuals can achieve greatness and inspire others to pursue their own dreams, regardless of the challenges they face. Her legacy continues to motivate people to overcome their own obstacles and reach their full potential, emphasizing the importance of empowerment over pity.

38. Charity Wrapped in Dignity!

Help the needy without hurting them.

Do you feel embarrassed bargaining in a designer hub? Do you feel obliged to give tips in an expensive restaurant? Do you feel the same hesitation or embarrassment while bargaining even for a penny when dealing with a local vendor, especially when those coins would mean nothing to you but would help in catering a day's meal for his family?

Well, we all know deep in our hearts the pointing harsh reality. Isn't it surprising that even the simple, noble, kind acts of charity in this era are not devoid of economic disparity?

We all talk a great deal about human rights, substantial development, kindness, and generosity. However, why our actions don't showcase the same virtues we talk so passionately about?

Proverbs like "Charity begins at home"; "Actions speak louder than words" are not mere words. It's imperative to understand the in-depth truth behind these words of wisdom. It's high time we understand the underlying truth behind our actions. A selfless act goes a long way in making us lead a meaningful life embodied with positivity and happiness.

While peeping into my childhood memories, one image that conjures up predominantly in my mind is that of my grandmother, a religious lady, walking down the street to a temple every morning draped in a snow-white saree with silver hairline and serene face speaking loud of years of experiences. Every morning I would watch my grandmother buying a lot of things from the local vendors sitting outside the temple. What surprised me the most was my grandmother buying things we neither needed nor were of much use! The same grandmother, my idol of wisdom, never failed to teach me the difference between what we need and what we want, who rather incessantly talked about spending wisely.

One day, on our way to the temple, I could not stop myself from asking her the reason for buying the things she did not require, rather poignantly. She certainly did not miss the underlying sarcasm in my tone. She smiled. What she said then has remained ever since embedded in my memories.

She said she wants to help the needy. She does not want to insult the needy and people who keep their self-respect before anything. She could have given some money without buying anything but she is respecting the labour of honest people without hurting their ego.

When we give selflessly, we add to the bank of good deeds that give us real inner peace and happiness.

39. Enjoy the Rhythm of Nature

The happiest thoughts that we have are the childhood memories of the time that we have spent in nature-bathing in the river, walking in lush green areas, and climbing the trees. There is harmony in nature. Mountains, brooks, canyons, green gardens, and sea beeches make us happy. If we spend time out in nature, we feel happy and relaxed. Why?

The answer is in the biophilia hypothesis.

"The biophilia hypothesis suggests that there is an instinctive bond between human beings and other living systems. Edward O. Wilson introduced and popularized the hypothesis in his book entitled *Biophilia.*

The term "biophilia" literally means "love of life or living systems." It was first used by Erich Fromm to describe a psychological orientation of being attracted to all that is alive and vital.

Philia is the opposite of phobia. In phobias, we have a fear of nature or natural surroundings, or other things. Philias are attraction towards nature and natural surroundings, positive feelings that we have towards certain habitats, activities, and objects in natural surroundings. We have a natural bond with nature. It is in our DNA. That is why humans feel attracted to nature, take care of nature, visit natural sights, and grow plants.

What do we get in nature? What do we learn from nature? We get solace in nature. We want to run from crowded and closed places, noise, and race to accumulate more and more wealth.

What do we get in nature?

Rhythm, harmony, and peace.

The sun rises and sets. The river flows from mountains, flows through plains, and joins the sea. There are fat trees, thin trees, and dry trees. All exist in harmony and all are beautiful. The birds, butterflies, and squirrels all move in perfect harmony. Nature teaches us to come out of our comfort zone. High mountains, the power of winds, vastness, and depth of the sea, all challenge us. We are amazed at the speed of wind, the vastness of the ocean, serene majesty of lofty mountains, and we realize the presence of the all-pervading Spirit. We feel solace in nature because our spirit meets the spirit of the Almighty in the lap of nature.

If we want to be happy, let us go close to nature because we have evolved from nature. Nature and we are made of the same elements. Japanese are known for living long and leading a happy life. The reason is their proximity to nature.

"The six best doctors: sunshine, water, rest, air, exercise, and diet."
– Wayne Fields

Nature has the key to happiness. The more we live naturally better will be our health. The more we go close to nature happier we will be. A single flower, the chirping of birds, the rustling sound of dry leaves when you walk over them, a cool breeze, a mild rain shower, and the sound of flowing water all can lift our mood. We all must enjoy and respect this gift of God-Nature to be happy. The peace and solace that we get when we are close to nature without spending a penny cannot be replaced by lofty, luxurious buildings or crowded malls. Money cannot buy peace and happiness but some minutes spent in nature can uplift our mood.

"Your health account, your bank account, they're the same thing. The more you put in, the more you can take out."

– *Jack LaLanne*

Source of image: Internet

40. Maintain Quality of Life

"The quality of life is more important than life itself." -Alexis Carrel

Quality of life (QOL) is defined by the World Health Organization as "an individual's perception of their position in life in the context of the culture and value systems in which they live and in relation to their goals, expectations, standards and concerns."

A healthy attitude towards life contributes to a good quality of life.

To fully appreciate all aspects of life, we must maintain a healthy mind and body. God has granted us each one life. Why damage it with negative thoughts? Give it your all, try your hardest, and then unwind. Never compare your situation to others in a negative way. Take pleasure in what you have. Continue to strive for more while maintaining harmony in your life.

An individual's quality of life (QOL) is assessed based on the meaningfulness, quality, and frequency of their daily activities. One should always be on the lookout for better choices, but one should also be content with the job that allows him to support himself financially. Feel content where you are if your circumstances prevent you from changing. Working while unhappy will be detrimental to your health.

"It's all about quality of life and finding a happy balance between work and friends and family." ~ Philip Green

Our mental attitude towards life is the greatest contributor to a good quality of life. As Jack Canfield has said "It is time to stop looking outside yourself for the answers to why you haven't created the life and results you want, for it is you who creates the quality of life you lead and the results you produce. You-no one else! To achieve major success in life-to achieve those things that are most important to you-you must assume 100% responsibility for your life.

Nothing less will do."

One such inspiring true story that reflects the essence of assuming responsibility for one's life is that of J.K. Rowling, the renowned author of the Harry Potter series. Before achieving literary success, Rowling faced numerous personal and professional setbacks. As a single mother living on welfare, she battled depression and financial instability while pursuing her passion for writing.

Despite the challenges, Rowling remained determined and persevered in her writing endeavors. Her mental attitude towards life, characterized by resilience and an unwavering belief in her abilities, propelled her to create the magical world of Harry Potter. Despite facing rejection from multiple publishers, Rowling persisted in her efforts, believing in the value of her work and the story she had to tell.

Through her perseverance and determination, Rowling eventually found a publisher for the first Harry Potter book, which went on to become an international sensation, captivating readers of all ages. Her success not only transformed her life but also inspired countless individuals worldwide to pursue their own dreams, regardless of the obstacles they may face.

J.K. Rowling's journey emphasizes the transformative power of taking full responsibility for one's life and choices. Despite the adversities she encountered, her unwavering commitment to her passion and her resolute attitude toward life ultimately led her to achieve extraordinary success. Her story serves as a powerful testament to the notion that our mental attitude and determination play a pivotal role in shaping the quality of life we lead and the outcomes we achieve.

41. Concentrate on True Quality

Value the values that are within you.

Six best friends made plans for a gathering at the residence of their favourite university professor, who had earned the admiration of many students and acted as a mentor to several of them during their university years. On the specified day, they all reached the professor's apartment as scheduled.

They were enjoying themselves, engaging in conversations about each other's whereabouts and advancements in their lives since their college graduation, and the paths that led them to their current situations. Some had achieved success as corporate executives, while a few had excelled as leaders, and others had become prosperous entrepreneurs. All of them were married and started families. Despite the initial quality of the discussion, it swiftly transformed into a session of grievances about work, relationships, stress, and the challenges of life.

At this point, the professor stepped in and gave everyone coffee. One thing was unusual. The coffee was served in different types of cups. Some cups were expensive and beautiful and some cups were plain.

Students thought that the professor did not have similar-looking cups in his home.

"Have you noticed, that all the excellent-looking and expensive cups are picked up, leaving behind the regular, simple, and inexpensive ones", the professor said as each of them held a cup. Surprisingly, no one noticed that there were extra cups of coffee, and once everyone had their cup, no one grabbed the ordinary cups, leaving them all on the serving tray.

The professor's insightful revelation soon followed. "Everyone gravitated towards the flashy cups, neglecting the ordinary ones?" he added. "While it's natural to seek the best for ourselves, this pursuit often underlies the majority of our troubles and anxieties in life."

Perplexed, the friends gazed at the professor, struggling to grasp the correlation between the choice of cups and life's stressors. Calmly, the professor continued, "Understand that the cup itself adds no value to the coffee. Often, it's merely an expensive façade, concealing the true essence within. What truly matters is the coffee, not the cup."

He further emphasized the need to savour life's experiences, emphasizing that while an attractive cup may enhance the visual appeal, it does not define the richness of the content it holds. What truly enriches life is the depth of experience, not the external embellishments.

Don't unbalance life while running after money, success, status, or valuable stuff. Always strive to live your life mindfully. The actual meaning of life is not worldly accomplishments, but going the extra mile in all you do.

Using unfair techniques in tests and in life increases stress. Living an ethical life is an accomplishment in itself. Staying on the right track is more satisfying than attaining achievement through unfair means. It will eventually derail you on your life's journey.

Remember that if life is a cup of coffee, then job, money,

prestige or social standing, and love, among other things, are the cups. They merely serve to hold and contain life. The type of cup we use does not define or alter the quality of our lives.

The heartfelt lesson lingered long after the gathering ended, prompting each friend to reflect on the true essence of their own lives. They realized that happiness isn't derived from material achievements but from the genuine contentment found within. As they departed, the friends carried with them a newfound appreciation for the beauty of life's simple joys and the genuine fulfilment found in embracing one's authentic self.

Source of image: Internet

42. Grow Up Actively

We often see an advertisement where a person is shown on a hospital bed and an insurance agent tells him he did not go for medical insurance and now his medical bill is rising. Let us put this in another way. Incorporate the "right to move" and habit to move into your lifestyle, thus maximizing the potential to maintain health and well-being in the most cost-effective and influential way possible.

Don't be a night owl, be an early bird, and find sufficient time for physical activities, that is the real investment. Without an active body, all your wealth will go to waste. Sweat during the day, maintain the mobility of your body, and remain blessed. Motivate yourself for long walks, and workouts, make this a regular habit, and enjoy life.Increased physical activity reduces health care costs and improves the productivity of the individual and the society. If we do physical activity in the right frame of mind, it has a triple benefit:

1- You are physically fit, and energetic, and can enjoy your life, and your wealth without the tension of diseases.

2- It improves the productivity of individuals and society, and you live a blissful life.

3- It is the best investment. Our physical health is like money. We value it when we have lost it.

It is never too late to select one of the two situations.

Situation One

You are sitting outside the chamber of your doctor and waiting for your turn with other ailing and worried patients, running from one part of the hospital to the other part reading signboards- Cardiology Ward, X-Ray, MRI, Blood Test, etc. How scary!

Situation Two

The other situation is you are out of your bed with the first ray of sun, listen to the chirping of the birds, feel the fragrance and freshness of nature, and do vigorous exercise and sweat. There is no fee for this.

Growing up actively and happily is the best investment in life. Good health is the gateway to happiness. Growing up actively is the key to that gateway.

Source of images: Internet

43. Live a Purposeful Life

"The purpose of life is not to be happy. It is to be useful, to be honourable, to be compassionate, to have it make some difference that you have lived and lived well." — Ralph Waldo Emerson

Hawking was diagnosed with Amyotrophic Lateral Sclerosis (ALS). As ALS progresses, the degeneration of motor neurons in the brain interferes with messages to muscle groups in the body. Eventually, muscle tissue atrophy and voluntary control of muscular tissues are lost.

When Stephe Hawking was only 21, his doctor told him, he is going to die. The sickness that generally comes with the age of 50, Stephen suffered at the age of 20. It was a clear sign that Stephen was going to die, He didn't have much time. But Stephen proved everyone wrong. Stephen lived for 76 years.

When confronted with the opportunity of early death, it makes you recognize that life is worth living. When he knew that he is going to die, Stephen decided not to live a purposeless life. It was the time that he decided to do something bigger in the field of science.

Realizing that life's fragility demands purpose, Hawking committed himself to a life of significance. Refusing to surrender to despair, he delved into the depths of scientific exploration, leaving an indelible mark on the world of theoretical physics. From groundbreaking research on the origins of the universe to unravelling the mysteries of black hole, Hawking's contributions reshaped our understanding of the cosmos.

His pursuit of knowledge extended beyond the scientific community, captivating the hearts and minds of readers worldwide through his bestselling books. Despite physical limitations, his intellectual prowess knew no bounds, inspiring generations to ponder the universe's complexities.

Stephen Hawking's story serves as a beacon of light, reminding us that even in the face of adversity, a life of purpose can transcend limitations. He proved that the human spirit, fuelled by determination and a relentless thirst for knowledge, can defy expectations and leave an enduring legacy. Though he departed this world at the age of 76, his impact continues to reverberate, cementing his place as one of the brightest minds in history and a testament to the power of living with purpose.

Have You Felt the Essence of What You Were Designed to Be?

According to Gregory Cootsona, "True success is to discern the essence of what we're created to be and to follow it relentlessly".

Have you experienced the true nature of who you were intended to be? If not, what is getting in the way of you? Lack of desire, perhaps? Are you not able to hear the whispers? Is it letting your hectic schedule trap you in a rut till your life becomes routine? Whatever is keeping you from feeling at home, know this: Until you find, unearth, or rediscover your divine mission and make it the centre of your life, you will never feel at home.

What purpose did God have for you and just you being here?

Every one of us has a goal. Each of us is present because we have work to do. We're all here with a call and work to complete. These insightful words beautifully sum up the purpose of life:

"If you are breathing, you are still alive. If you are alive, then you are still here, physically, on this planet. If you are still here, then you have not completed what you were put on earth to do. If you have not completed what you were put on earth to do…that means your very purpose has not yet been fulfilled. If your purpose has not yet been fulfilled, then the most important part of your life has not yet been lived..."(Andy Andrews, *The Noticer*, pp. 84-5.) No matter how old or young or tired or sad or busy or lazy or whatever we believe ourselves to be, we all have work to do.

Purpose and Meaning Are the Secrets to True Happiness

According to research, finding meaning and purpose in life is what leads to the happiest people. According to Martin Seligman, Ph.D., the founder of positive psychology, many people lead a "pleasant life," which consists of frequently having happy emotions. Sure, it's important to feel good, to have fun, and to enjoy life, but if you actually want it, there's much more that should be added.

"The engaged life" includes more than just feeling well; it also includes a focus on character, a sense of being actively involved in life, and a genuine desire to better yourself and be the best. And that's also rather good; it's surely more desirable than leading a merely comfortable life. The "meaningful life" is the ultimate goal, nevertheless. In addition to generating happy emotions and being active, these people also build what Seligman refers to as "meaningful positive institutions," or, in other words, they lead meaningful lives.

Once upon a time in a quaint little village, there lived a wise old storyteller named Mahaveer. He was known far and wide for his captivating tales that touched the hearts of those who listened. He had a secret, one that he only shared with a few trusted friends.

Every evening, as the sun dipped below the horizon, Mahaveer would take a small wooden boat out to a serene lake nestled deep in the forest. He would light an earthen lamp and set it afloat on the water, watching it drift away until it was a mere flicker in the distance. Mahaveer believed that each lamp carried a piece of his soul, and this ritual was his way of sharing his essence with the world.

As the years passed, word of Mahaveer's earthen lamp ritual spread throughout the village. People came from near and far to witness this nightly event.

One evening, a curious young girl named Amla approached Mahaveer and asked him, "Why do you do this?" Mahaveer smiled and said, "Amla, the lamp represents the stories I've told and the emotions I've shared. They carry my hopes, my dreams, and my love. I believe that by setting them free, I can make the world a bit brighter."

Amla was deeply moved by this and asked, "How can I live a life as meaningful as yours? "Mahaveer paused, then replied, "Find what you love and share it with the world. Whether it's through stories, acts of kindness, or your unique talents, your contribution will be like a lantern, lighting up the lives of those around you."

Amla returned to her home inspired by Mahaveer's words. She discovered her love for gardening and began tending a neglected community garden. She shared the fruits of her labour with her neighbours, distributed saplings to villagers and soon, the garden bloomed with not only flowers but also a sense of community feeling and joy.

Years later, Amla became known as "The Garden Storyteller", and her village thrived with shared stories, love, and the beauty of her garden. She continued Mahaveer's tradition by launching earthen lamps into the same serene lake, sharing her own piece of the world with others.

Mahaveer and Amla's story reminds us that a meaningful life is not just about personal achievements, but about how we touch the lives of those around us. It's about finding what we love and sharing it, like lanterns on a tranquil lake, casting light on the darkness and bringing warmth to the hearts of others.

As long as you're alive, you have a purpose. You might as well pull it out, put it on, and let it shine. Your purpose, your life's mission, your calling—whatever you want to call it—is as long as you're alive. "The way you get meaning into your life is to devote yourself to loving others, devote yourself to your community around you, and devote yourself to creating something that gives you purpose and meaning." Mitch Album

Living purposeful life is the key to happiness.

44. Happiness

Our soul is Sat-Chit-Anand. It is full of happiness because it comes from the infinite source of joy--God. Give this enjoyment to others, and you will feel immense satisfaction and fulfillment.

A lecture was once attended by 50 participants. The speaker abruptly stopped and began handing out balloons to each person. Each person was instructed to use a marker pen to write his/her name on the item. The balloons were then gathered and placed in a different room.

These delegates were then permitted entry into the other room and given five minutes to locate the balloon bearing their names. There was complete mayhem as everyone scurried about looking for their names, bumping into one another, and pushing people aside.

After five minutes, nobody could locate the balloon. Each person was then instructed to choose a balloon at random and present it to the person whose name had been printed on it.

Everyone had their balloon in no time. This is exactly what is happening in our life, the speaker said. Everyone is feverishly searching for happiness everywhere but doesn't know where to find it.Our happiness lies in the happiness of other people. Give them their happiness; you will get your happiness. And this is the purpose of human life.

Essence of Happiness: Small things matter

The four lines of the poem "Little Things" by Julia Carney hold the essence of happiness.

> *"Little deeds of kindness,*
> *Little words of love,*
> *Make our earth happy,*
> *Like the Heaven above."*

Positive communication is the key to happiness.

The art of communication may be a common source of conflict among friends, relations, and co-workers. you'll bleed an individual with unkind and sarcastic words, otherwise, you can soothe another person's feelings with sweet and kind words. John and Julie Gottman conducted 40 years of relationship research and concluded that small words, small gestures, and little acts are the key factors for happy relationships everywhere.

Keep communication positive. Maintain a positive tone in your communication. Those who are happy and successful keep a 20: 1 ratio of positive to negative expressions. Don't ignore or respond with anger to the needs of the other person. Instead "turn towards" the other person. Turning towards the attention of the other person means paying attention to the needs of others, and connecting with positive expressions. Each time we express love, appreciation, and respect for others we receive the same from the other person. Small positive acts are the key to a happy relationship. "Turning towards" the other person can be done either verbally or non-verbally; with warmth, humour, affection, complimenting each other, or emphasizing the good things. Giving a hug and kiss when greeting each other, saying "I love you". These small positive acts done often are key to a happy and healthy relationship.

An example of "turning away"/rude response:

I lost my father. Before proceeding to the funeral, I had to inform my boss. I was very emotional and sad. I was shocked by the response from my boss. I was expecting some soothing words like "Sorry to learn about the demise of your father. We are with you in this hour of grief." She said nothing like this. Her prompt reaction was- "He was old and ailing. Time for him to go". What does it show? Crude behaviour, poor upbringing, and negative communication.

Example of "turning towards": A more positive and comforting form of communication could have been, "I am deeply sorry to hear about his passing. May his soul rest in peace, and may you find the strength to endure this profound loss. Please do not hesitate to reach out to us for anything you might need. We are here to support you during this challenging time." While I understand that my father cannot be brought back, compassionate words and kind words would have embalmed my feelings.

The tone of communication is a common source of conflict for many friends. What can be done to improve it? Why are the same fights taking place over and over? With healthy communication, how can friends and partners have a happy relationship? The secret, according to experts is to do small things frequently.

Small words, small gestures, and small acts help to build long-term relationships. Tips for having positive communication and happy long-term relationships include:
- Turning towards people rather than away from them.
- Remember someone in distress has approached you expecting kind words, good advice, suggestions, or material help.
- To de-stress, engage in a minimum 20-minute conversation in person, via message, or over the phone.
- Maintain an interest in friends and family.

Always remember that small gestures, small words, and small acts of kindness count in life. Today someone has approached, you ,tomorrow you may need the help of others.

Source of image: Internet

45. Making Connections -Kintsugi Style

Similar to a cherished cup or plate, individuals may sometimes develop cracks as a result of challenging circumstances, or even break entirely. It is crucial that we refrain from discarding ourselves when faced with such challenges. Instead, we can acquire the ability to transform these imperfections into blessings, much like the ancient Japanese art of kintsugi, which embellishes fractured pottery. As we mature, we encounter numerous difficulties and fluctuations in our circumstances. During trying times, let us remember that losses can be repaired, situations can be improved, and life can be celebrated in a manner reminiscent of the art of Kintsugi.

Kintsugi, also known as kintsukuroi, is the Japanese art of mending broken pottery with lacquer dusted or mixed with powdered gold, silver, or platinum; the method is similar to the maki-e technique. It views breakage and repair as part of an object's history, rather than as something to conceal.

Most people do not intentionally break their prized pieces of pottery, but this is not always the case in Japanese culture. Beautifying broken ceramics with lacquer mixed with powdered gold is a more than 500-year-old Japanese tradition that emphasizes rather than hides imperfections. This not only teaches patience when a prized piece of pottery breaks, but it also serves as a reminder of the beauty of human frailty.

Human relationships are also as delicate as a delicate piece of pottery.

The Japanese do not conceal broken pieces. They make it beautiful and proudly display it. We, like a piece of pottery, break due to circumstances, but there is a lesson for us to learn. Instead of feeling rejected and defeated, we can transform adversity into opportunity and emerge victorious.

In a world that so often values youth and perfection, it may appear strange to embrace the old and battered. However, the 15th-century practice of kintsugi, which means "to join with gold," is a reminder to remain optimistic when things fall apart and to celebrate life's flaws and missteps.

The kintsugi technique is an extension of the Japanese wabi-sabi philosophy, which sees beauty in the imperfect and value in simplicity. The gilded restoration of the broken pieces can take up to three months because the fragments are carefully glued together with the sap of an indigenous Japanese tree, allowed to dry for a few weeks, and then adorned with gold running along its cracks.

In our day-to-day life patience is required for coming out of a difficult situation. Bad things and bad times do not remain forever. By being optimistic, patient, and self-healing, things do improve. Learning to accept and cherish scars and faults is a valuable lesson in sustainability and humanity in an age of mass production and quick disposal. At times relations become sour due to differences or hardship. Let us try to heal and come out victorious from such situations. Every relationship can be mended with positivity and patience.

Source of image: Internet

46. Social Support

Can we live alone?

Can we sort out all the problems alone?

The answer to both questions is no. We are social beings. There are times when we all require social support.

Do you have someone you can talk to when you need support in your life? When your basement floods or you need someone to monitor the kids, who can you call? Or perhaps just a phone number you can call when something truly wonderful occurs and you want to tell someone?

Your friends, family, coworkers, and other people can provide you with social support in the form of both physical and emotional comfort. It is an awareness that you are a part of a group of individuals who value you, admire, and care about you.

What is social support?

Social support means having friends and other people, including family, to turn to in times of need or crisis. It provides you with a wider focus and a positive self-image. Social support improves the quality of life and acts as a protective barrier against unfavourable life circumstances.

Types of Social Support

Emotional support

When someone listens to you, has empathy for you, and expresses concern for you, they are being emotionally supportive. For instance, if you lost your job or separated from your partner a close friend might give you physical consolation by hugging you or calling you every day during the first few weeks to check on you.

Physical Support

People who care about you might provide you with services or practical support, such as financial or food presents, or assistance in another form. You have shifted to a new house, and this type of assistance enables you to do daily duties and reduces some of the burdens.

Expressing Faith in You

Some individuals support you by expressing their faith in you or by motivating you. They might assist you in maintaining an optimistic and rational perspective of the situation and remind you of your strengths. Before a crucial presentation at school, for instance, a classmate can point up your communication skills and prior achievements.

Sharing Information

When relatives, friends, or even professionals provide real information or offer their opinions on a specific situation, it can be pretty beneficial. For instance, a friend who has joined a professional course before you can provide details on the cost of the tuition fee, lodging and boarding expenditure, and advice on sticking to a budget, or a person who has previously lost their job might share resources for networking or advice on how to look for new employment.

"A best friend is the only one that walks into your life when the world has walked out." — Shannon L. Alder

We all need support. We all need people who care and understand us. We need honest, nurturing, loving, and supportive relationships to survive. Having friends and other people, such as family, to turn to in times of need or disaster offer us a buffer against unfavourable life occurrences. Social support is needed to improve the quality of life.

47. Our Journey Together Is So Short

"Our journey together is so brief."
A lovely message for all of us
A young lady was traveling by train. A loud and grumpy old lady arrived at the next station and sat beside her. She crammed into the seat and banged into her with her numerous bags.

The person seated on the opposite side of the young lady became irritated and questioned why she didn't speak up and say something.

The young lady smiled, "The ride together is so short; it is not necessary to be rude or fight over something so minor. "At the next station, I'll get off."

This response ought to be written in gold letters:
"It is unnecessary to argue over something so trivial; our journey together is so short."

If each of us realizes that our time here is so limited and that it would be a waste of time and energy to waste it with quarrels, fruitless fights, not forgiving others, unhappiness, and a fault-finding mindset.
Did someone cause you heartbreak? Keep cool; the journey is short.
Has someone betrayed, bullied, cheated, or humiliated you? Be patient and forgiving; the journey is short.
Whatever problems someone gives us, let us keep in mind that our journey together is so brief.

Nobody knows how long this voyage will take. Nobody knows when they will come to an end. Our journey together has been so brief. Let us treasure our friends and family. Let us be courteous, respectful, and forgiving to one another. Let us be filled with gratitude and joy.

If I have ever injured you, please forgive me. You already have my forgiveness if you have ever hurt me.

After all, our time together is so brief!

Source of image: Internet

48. Be a Real Hero

"Heroes are made by the paths they choose, not the power they are graced with." – Brodi Ashton

A true story about real heroes.

In a horrific case of animal cruelty, a man tied a dog to his car and mercilessly dragged it around the city. The incident took place in Rajasthan's Jodhpur district.

A video of the incident shows the man, who is a doctor by profession, driving the car while the chained dog struggles to keep up with the running car. A person on the bike spotted the animal abuse and immediately reacted and made the driver stop the car. The locals unchained the dog and informed the city's Dog Home Foundation about the incident. The locals also arranged for an ambulance for the severely injured dog. A case has been registered against the doctor under the Animal Cruelty Act.

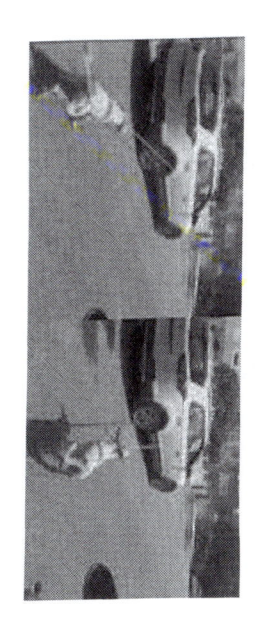

What does this incident convey? This incident serves as a poignant reminder that professional titles do not necessarily reflect one's true character, as the doctor's actions stood in stark contrast to the compassion exhibited by the concerned citizens who rushed to aid the distressed animal. While the doctor failed to uphold a moral standard, these unnamed individuals demonstrated qualities of true heroism. It is crucial to recognize that heroic behaviour stems from traits such as empathy, nurturance, and a commitment to ethical principles.

While it is commendable to extend help to those in need, it is important to exercise caution and consider one's own limitations before engaging in risky rescue attempts. Training and expertise play a vital role in effectively managing challenging situations, as demonstrated by individuals with specialized skills such as first aid responders. It is not wise to jump into deep water to save someone when you do not know swimming.

Persistence is yet another hallmark of heroism, as genuine heroes persist in their endeavours despite encountering failures. A 2010 study highlighted the tendency of real heroes to find positive outcomes in adverse circumstances, fostering a deeper appreciation for life and fostering connections with those they assist. By cultivating empathy, competence, and perseverance over time, one can enhance their capacity to assist others and achieve success in their endeavours.

49. Focus on positive

"Reframing is a term from cognitive psychotherapy which simply means seeing something in a new way, in a new context, with a new frame around it." - Elaine N. Aron

Positive Reframing technique

Find a silver lining in the storm clouds above. Positive reframing technique can assist in regaining control of our mindset. Positive thinking does not mean denying that problems exist, pretending there is no problem, or failing to conceive of workable solutions. Rather, it involves turning your negative thoughts into positive ones by seeing the bright side and searching for a silver lining in the ominous clouds overhead. Reframing won't change the actual outcome of a situation, but it can change the way you feel about your circumstances. It involves putting a more positive spin on your negative thoughts.

Say you slipped in wet leaves and fell off your bike while training for a race. You didn't sustain any life-threatening injuries, but you did sprain your ankle. This confined you to bed for several weeks, leaving you disappointed and irritated with yourself for riding carelessly.

Blaming yourself will likely only make you feel worse. Self-compassion, however, can help you accept the disappointment in stride and turn your attention toward your next opportunity. Maybe you praise yourself for always making sure to wear your helmet, tell yourself you'll be better prepared for the race next year, or feel grateful you didn't break anything else.

50. Overcoming Stress and Anxiety- Vedic Approach

Chinta denotes mental trepidations, worry, or anxiety about something that is going to happen. Chinta is responsible for the mind becoming preoccupied with ideas that cause anxiety, fear, pressure, and sleeplessness. Your mind is shadowed by fear paralyzing your capability to think. It is a negative trait that can significantly hinder the mind's ability to notice, think, plan, and act. A person absorbed in Chinta may misinterpret an opportunity for a threat and a risk for a chance.

Kapil, a robust and healthy professional, experienced a sudden collapse while exercising at the gym. He was swiftly transported to the nearby nursing home, where he received prompt medical attention and underwent thorough examinations. Anticipating his medical results, he grappled with worry, making it challenging to focus on positive thoughts. Nonetheless, the timely access to proper medical care turned out to be a blessing in disguise, marking the early detection of a severe ailment that could be effectively treated in its initial stages. This incident serves as a testament to how mental anxieties, apprehensions, and distress can significantly impact an individual's cognitive abilities and mental peace.

Nevertheless, attaining such mental composure is easier said than done. Even the most revered sages in Vedic scriptures struggled to conquer their inner turmoil. Sustaining unwavering mental equilibrium proves to be demanding, especially when one's attention is focused on specific expectations and outcomes.

Krishna proposed in the Bhagavad Gita:

कर्मण्येवाधिकारस्ते माफलेषुकदाचन

TAMING THE MONKEY MIND

Maintain your concentration on your actions and responsibilities without worrying about the outcome.

Most individuals find it difficult to follow this basic suggestion. "How can one prepare for success without worrying about it?" they ask. Krishna suggests in Shrimad Bhagwat Gita that we "stop worrying" about the consequences, but not to stop thinking about them. Worrying is optional, whereas thinking is vital.

Thoughts are of three kinds, सत्व Satva or Satvic, रजो Rajo or Rajas, and तमो Tamo or Tamas. Rajo or Rajasic thoughts are those that are immersed in dread with partial rationality and focus.

When our thoughts are completely consumed by fear and lack any kind of hope, we have a Tamas or Tamasic thought.

Chinta is represented by both Rajasic and Tamasic concepts. When Chinta overwhelms the mind, it begins to reflect on our bodies. Signs like trembling legs, high palpitation, and dry mouth, are physical signs that we are overwhelmed by Chinta.

It is therefore important that we remove all remnants of Chinta from our thinking. And only via Chintan, or conscious thinking or contemplation, is this possible.

The four main roles of the mind are to observe, understand, think, and act. Chinta-affected minds cannot often understand and think. It is a travesty that humans, who pride themselves on their ability to reason, have frequently acted more on impulse, only to make their lives miserable.

The majority of people think that having money will solve all of their issues, and they will do anything to get it. When they do receive it, however, a lot of people say that it is "inadequate" or "too difficult to manage."

When you are having a problem, take a break. Instead of grumbling about it, find a quiet place. Close your eyes and think about the problem. There should not be any traces of passion, anger, greed, infatuation, ego, or envy. After you have fully explained the situation, think about potential solutions. Then, before developing that solution, think about its limitations. Once you've come up with a clear solution, balance your thoughts and get to work without overthinking the result. Instead of worrying, think about modifying your strategy.

Consider improving your approach and continuing to look for ways to enhance your work and yourself. And never do something without first thinking about it thoroughly. When you can think and work together, you are in the Chintan-Manthan process - a constant churning of positive thoughts. Wherever you are, you are always objective; rarely subjective. (Prabhu,2021)

Part Five
Spiritual Orientation

51. What Is Spirituality?

Spirituality is not having faith in a belief system or path, being a Hindu, a Christian, a Muslim, a Parsi, or a Sikh. There are hundreds of ways to experience spirituality, live in spirituality, or feel spirituality. We are not only mind, flesh, and bones. We have spirit also. The viewpoint offered by spirituality suggests that there is more to life than just what people can physically and sensory experience, something greater that connects all beings and to the universe itself. "Inside us there is something that has no name, that something is what we are."- José Saramago

Spirituality is finding purpose in life, feeling happy beyond external rewards and material possessions, and wanting to make the world a better place. You don't have to go round the globe to make earth a better place, you make a place happy by finding happiness and peace right with the people you are living with. Spirituality and happiness are contagious. It has undercurrents. The company, thoughts, and deeds of a spiritual being leave an impact on anyone, who comes in contact with him. He is like a candle that can light many other candles.

Spirituality Has Different Meaning for Different People

- For some spirituality is belief in supreme power. When we start a new work, we seek the blessings of God.
- For others, it is connectedness with the rest of humanity. That is why we are moved to see people in distress in other parts of the world. War is going on in Ukraine, we feel connected with the people who are suffering. We are moved to see the destruction of houses, and infrastructure, wounded and dead, people who are forced to leave their houses.

- For some spirituality is to know the feeling of wonder and awe seeing the wonders of nature, the serenity of nature, the movement of waves and clouds, twinkling of stars in the sky.
- Seeking happiness beyond material possessions or other external rewards is spirituality. A tribesman, who lives with his community, eats together, lives together, and connects with his people is happier than a billionaire who has a palace, wealth, and a jet of his own, who many a time feels uncomfortable about his ranking in the richest people, value of his stock, his position, and false prestige.
- Spirituality is seeking meaning and purpose in life in contrast to living a selfish life with a self-centred attitude toward me and only me. Simple village people jump to save the drowning people without any selfish motive, and many a time they lose their life, this is spirituality.
- Spirituality is wanting to make the world a better place, in whatever capacity, experiencing compassion and empathy for others, feeding the hungry, sharing what you have showing empathy for those who are needy and suffering.

Spirituality and emotional well-being are closely linked.

Spirituality is all about seeking a deep connection with something greater than yourself, which can result in good feelings like calm, wonder, contentment, gratitude, and acceptance. Emotional wellness is all about developing a positive attitude, broadening your perspective, and recognizing and incorporating a connection to something greater than yourself, that is why emotional well-being and spirituality are connected and intricately integrated. People having spiritual orientation are emotionally healthy.

Story of Alex: In the bustling city of Metropolis, amidst the chaos of modern life, there existed a peculiar little café named "Soul Brew." Its walls were adorned with calming shades of blue and earthy green, and the aroma of freshly ground coffee beans intermingled with the scent of incense, creating an atmosphere that beckoned one to pause and reflect.

At the heart of this sanctuary was Ruby, a barista with an enigmatic aura. Her eyes, pools of serenity, seemed to hold a thousand untold stories. Every morning, she greeted her customers with a genuine smile, and her mere presence had a way of calming even the most restless souls.

One stormy evening, a troubled young executive named Alex stumbled into Soul Brew, seeking solace from the relentless pressures of his high-powered job. As he sank into a worn-out armchair, he noticed Ruby's gentle gaze enveloping him like a warm embrace. She approached him with a mug of steaming chai, infused with a pinch of cardamom powder, and a touch of tranquility.

"Rough day?" Ruby asked softly, her voice carrying a soothing melody.

Alex hesitated, but something in her demeanour encouraged him to open up. He told her about the endless demands of his career, the sense of disconnect from his true self, and the relentless pursuit of success that left him feeling hollow. Ruby listened intently, her understanding gaze conveying a profound empathy that seemed to transcend words.

With a reassuring smile, she shared her own journey of self-discovery, how she had found solace in the teachings of ancient philosophies and the practice of mindfulness. "The key," she explained, "lies in nurturing the spirit. When we connect with something greater than ourselves, be it through prayer, meditation, or simply communing with nature, we open the door to inner peace and emotional well-being."

In the days that followed, Alex found himself drawn back to

Soul Brew, not just for the aromatic beverages, but for the heartfelt conversations that left him feeling understood and uplifted. With Ruby's guidance, he delved into the realms of spirituality, exploring various practices that spoke to his soul. He learned to embrace moments of stillness, to find gratitude in the simple joys of life, and to seek meaning beyond the materialistic pursuits that had once consumed him.

Spirituality and Religion

Religion is practiced in a particular community, based on a specific set of rules and customs, having belief in deities, religious text, and tradition. Spirituality can be practiced individually, without adhering to a specific set of rules. A person with a spiritual orientation focuses on a personal journey of discovering what is right and meaningful in life. A person can have a spiritual orientation without being a member of a particular sect.

"Spirituality is such a positive aspect of human life and excellence that we must hold it in high regard." Spirituality is good for our physical, social, and emotional wellness. It fosters harmony, serenity, and contentment. Positive thinking, internal serenity, ego lessness, unconditional love, optimism, harmony, humility, responsibility, compassion, justice, simplicity, and reciprocity are traits of a spiritually oriented individual. These traits allow us to live our lives wholly and happily.

Source of image: Internet

52. Be a Person of substance and spiritual Orientation

"The two most important days in your life are the day you are born and the day you find out why."- Mark Twain

We meet hundreds of people in our life. Do we remember everyone? No. We remember a few. Not necessarily they belong to high society, affluent, educated in foreign universities. The person can be a gardener, driver, butler, colleague, boss, teacher, relative, elderly person, or can be anyone we have come across. Some people leave an impression on us. We remember them, we talk about them. They are people of substance because of their, thoughts, actions, and deeds.

A person of substance is an individual who possesses substance and has a strong sense of self, values, and purpose in life. These people are genuine and authentic, and their actions align with their beliefs. They prioritize personal growth, strive for meaningful connections, and make a positive impact in their own lives and the lives of others. By focusing on substance rather than superficial qualities, individuals can live a more fulfilling and purposeful life.

I am a person of substance

"I am a person of substance. Don't judge me by my looks or my clothes. I am more than what meets the eye. Define me by the tough battles I fight each day. Define me by my courage to face them as I rise above no matter how difficult. My life is not glorious and I don't have medals to flaunt but my biggest trophy is my heart full of love and compassion. I value love, friendship, honesty, and trust. I am a person of substance and I will survive despite all odds in my life because I am strong through and through." (https://lessonslearnedinlife.com)

A shallow person vs. a person of substance

A shallow person is someone who lacks significant depth. A man of substance is emotionally and intellectually sound. A shallow person is someone who lacks vision and has just a superficial understanding of issues. Such a person cannot command respect in the family, workplace, or society.

We come into contact with a wide variety of people every day. some of them we admire, others we dislike, some we avoid. What type of person we want to be is a question we should ask ourselves frequently.

We should consider ourselves a student, someone who is still learning how to get around in this world, how to connect with it, and where we fit in it, even if we may be fully grown-up adults. The process of constant self-discovery makes life worth living. We should strive every day to become a person of substance. If we can fulfil this goal in everyday life, we will have accomplished something valuable at the moment. Remember, self-discovery is a personal journey, and everyone's process may look different. Stay open-minded and embrace the changes and growth that come from continuous self-discovery.

Who is a Person of Substance?
A person of substance adds value to the world.

He wants to make the world better; in whatever capacity he can do. He creates something, whether it be something material, an idea, or a feeling. He puts forth a lot of effort, and he succeeds. Such people can be either thinkers or doers. They are real and true. They are genuine.

Arrange a death bed test for yourself.

Imagine you are dead. People are sitting around your body. How many of them are remembering you for something good you have done for them?

I have read the story of a professor. He attended the funeral ceremony of his friend. People were reading funeral speeches, speaking from the heart praising the person after his death. A unique idea struck him. He thought what is the point of reading pages in praise of someone when he cannot listen? So, he arranged a living funeral for himself and asked his friends and students to read whatever they had to say for him. Everyone mentioned whatever he has done for them-helping them in their research, guiding them in trouble, and lending help when they were in financial crises. He died the next day!

We all are unique. We all have talent. Why not share it and live a purposeful life? Why not live a life that people remember you? Why not be a person of substance?

Traits of a person of substance:
They do activities that keep them happy and alive.
They consistently find time for activities that give them a Sense of happiness and aliveness.
Oprah Winfrey: A prominent media personality and philanthropist, Winfrey has been a powerful advocate for a range of social issues, including education, poverty, and women's rights. She has used her platform to inspire and uplift others through her television shows, books, and charitable initiatives.
There is no upper or lower limit of learning for them. They are always hungry for knowledge.
They always add and contribute
People of Substance attract people's attention. People of Substance offer something for the betterment of the world.
Jane Goodall: A renowned primatologist and conservationist, Goodall has dedicated her life to studying and protecting chimpanzees in Tanzania and advocating for environmental conservation. She has made significant contributions to the understanding of animal behaviour and has been a strong advocate for wildlife conservation.

They have their work ethics and are always ready to roll up their sleeves to help someone or get some work done. They are people of principles. People of Substance work hard and it shows.

Nelson Mandela: An influential leader and anti-apartheid activist, Mandela fought tirelessly against racial segregation in South Africa. He dedicated his life to the pursuit of justice and equality and became the country's first black president.

They are creative and imaginative and believe in making something. They push themselves out of their comfort zone.

They embrace nuance and uncertainty. They acknowledge that virtually everything in life is full of complications. The world is not black and white - it is shades of grey. People of substance can see the other side of every argument, perhaps because they want to experience the world through someone else's eyes, however briefly.

They are curious, dig into the details, and ask questions. People of Substance want more than just a soundbite of information on a particular topic. They're curious and want to learn as much as possible.

They value books like they value air, food, and water. Reading is the lifeline of the person of substance.

One of the easiest ways to be a Person of Substance is to aid another human being in some way. It also puts positive energy out into the universe. When other people see you helping out, they are also motivated to help and it creates a positive, upward spiral of well-being.

They do not take any shortcuts. People of Substance want to see things through to the end. They believe that experience is in the journey, not the destination.

Life isn't about checking things off a list - it's about experiencing life to its fullest at the moment, in good moments and bad. That is how we learn, that is how we grow, that is how we become the best people of substance we can be. (Shawber, 2019)

We all can be a person of substance. We all can add value to the world. We don't have to be a scientist, or a writer for adding value. Our simple thoughts and deeds add value to the world. Giving food to a hungry person, assisting someone in difficult hours, sharing your talent for the benefit of others, spreading positivity, and ensuring that we are in the world with a purpose. If we wish we all can make this place a better place by adding value here. Many people come and go but we remember a few because of this quality of theirs. We all arrived in the world with some purpose. Let us not waste our life. Be a person of substance.

Part Six

Words of wisdom and values from Shrimad Bhagavad Gita

53. About Shrimad Bhagavad Gita

Shrimad Bhagavad Gita is a Hindu scripture from the second century BCE that is part of the epic Mahabharata. The scripture contains a lot of positive and beneficial vibes that help us in our spiritual journey. The Shrimad Bhagavad Gita comprises of 18 chapters and contains 700 Sanskrit shlokas that explain the philosophy of life. It is a collection of dialogues between Arjuna, the Pandeva prince, and Lord Krishna during the Kurukshetra battle. This Hindu sacred book highlights the core values of life that have inspired the past generations, are inspiring the present generations, and will inspire the future generations. It has universal appeal.

Lord Krishna gave Arjuna the message of Shrimad Bhagavad Gita as advice on what is right and wrong when Arjuna was hesitant to go to war against his cousins the Kauravas, teachers, and relations.

The Bhagavad Gita discusses different spiritual methods such as right behaviour (Karma Yoga), devotion (Bhakti Yoga), and wisdom (Jnana Yoga).

We will be discussing the symbolic significance behind the chariot image and some valuable and practical Bhagavad Gita quotations. These quotes are still relevant today and can genuinely help us improve our quality of life.

54. Symbolic Significance of the Chariot Image in the Shrimad Bhagavad Gita

Shri Krishna imparts Arjun several spiritual lessons in the Shrimad Bhagavad Gita. The symbolism behind the chariot image, which depicts Arjun, Krishna, and the five horses driving the chariot is like this:

1. The chariot symbolizes the physical body.

2. Each of the five horses represents one of our senses: sight, hearing, taste, touch, and smell.

3. The reins represent the mind. Our minds are linked to our senses and can control them.

4. The charioteer indicates intelligence.

5. The soul is represented by the traveller.

6. Krishna is the supreme soul.

Our purpose in life as humans, according to this symbolism, is to use our mind and intellect to steer the chariot (body) to its destination. The ultimate goal is to fully understand life, live a meaningful existence, and achieve enlightenment.

55. Some Lessons from the Shrimad Bhagavad Gita

Remain calm

The biggest lesson of the Bhagavad Gita is to remain calm in all circumstances. In the middle of war and panic, Shri Krishna gave to the world the philosophy of righteous conduct.

सञ्जय उवाच। तं तथा कृपयाविष्टमश्रुपूर्णाकुलेक्षणम्। विषीदन्तमिदं वाक्यमुवाच मधुसूदनः ॥ 1 ॥

Meaning: In this manner, when Arjuna was plunged in a state of despondency, with eyes blurred with tears, Lord Krishna addressed these words to him.

Source of image: Internet

Come Over Mental Weakness: Undoubtedly, kindness is a great quality. But there are times when being compassionate turns into mental weakness. It is not noble in human nature to feel pity after deciding to wage a just battle to uphold the Dharma; rather, it is a weak mental condition that cannot withstand the pressure of responsibility and righteous action. A just fight for the sake of justice is required of the Kshatriya. Arjun was a kshatriya. He was duty-bound to fight for the right cause. He felt weak when he saw his close relatives, friends, and teachers in the battleground, the Lord guided him in his moment of weakness. There are times when there is a need to make difficult decisions for the sake of the greater good.

न त्वेवाहं जातु नासं न त्वं नेमे जनाधिपाः। न चैव न भविष्यामः सर्वे वयमतः परम्॥2.12॥

Meaning: I am never born, and I never die; neither you nor these kings have ever existed before, nor will any of us cease to exist in the future.

Interpretation: In this verse, Lord Krishna is explaining that our true essence, our soul, is eternal and does not undergo birth or death. He is telling Arjuna that neither he, nor the other warriors on the battlefield, nor himself, have ever truly been born or will ever truly die. Instead, they all exist eternally, and their physical forms are temporary manifestations.

This teaching is meant to convey the idea of the eternal nature of the soul and the impermanence of the physical body. It encourages Arjuna to overcome his fear of fighting in the battle because, ultimately, the soul cannot be harmed or destroyed.

This teaching instills immense strength and bravery. When a person realizes that he and others fundamentally do not perish, there is no reason for sorrow. Death is then seen as merely a transition of identity and appearance. Just as a seed breaks apart and grows into a plant. Although the seed's name and form vanish, it continues to exist as a plant. Lord Krishna identified the underlying cause of Arjuna's grief and understood that knowledge of the Atma (Soul) alone could eliminate all weakness and despair. Therefore, he begins his instruction with a powerful affirmation of the immortality of the soul and the eternal nature of individual beings.

देहिनोऽस्मिन्यथा देहे कौमारं यौवनं जरा।तथा देहान्तरप्राप्तिर्धीरस्तत्र न मुह्यति ॥2.13॥

Meaning: Just as the soul within this body goes through childhood, youth, and old age, it similarly passes into another body after death. A wise person is not bewildered by this.

Interpretation: In this Bhagavad Gita verse, Shri Krishna establishes the principle of reincarnation of the soul from one life to another. He explained that throughout life, our bodies progress from childhood to youth to maturity and then to old age. Modern science tells us that cells in the body renew, old cells die, and are replaced by new cells. It is estimated that almost every cell in the body will be renewed within seven years. Additionally, molecular changes in cells occur faster. From a scientific perspective, approximately ninety-eight percent of the molecules in our body change in a year. No matter how much our bodies change, we still think we're the same person because we are not the material body, but the soul that lives within us.

The soul changes bodies multiple times in a single lifetime since the body is always evolving. Similarly, when someone dies, it enters another body. In reality, what we commonly refer to as "death" is simply the soul getting rid of its old, defective body, and what we typically refer to as "birth" is the soul getting a new body somewhere else. This is the reincarnation theory.

In essence, Shloka 2.13 encourages students to see life as a continuous journey, understand the impermanence of the physical body, and cultivate wisdom to transcend the fear of death. It promotes a holistic perspective on life that encourages responsible living and personal growth beyond the physical realm.

मात्रास्पर्शास्तु कौन्तेय शीतोष्णसुखदु: खदा: |
आगमापायिनोऽनित्यास्तांस्तितिक्षस्व भारत ||2.14||

Meaning: O son of Kunti, the contact between the senses and the sense objects gives rise to fleeting perceptions of happiness and distress. These are non-permanent and come and go like the winter and summer seasons. O descendent of Bharat, one must learn to tolerate them without being disturbed.

Interpretation: This verse from the Bhagavad Gita conveys an exceptionally strong and significant message that nothing in this life is permanent. Summers and winters are only temporary. It comes and goes over time. Similarly pleasure and pain pass away, they are both transient.

Life will have its ups and downs, difficult moments, and challenging circumstances. Be patient and develop the ability to put up with things while being unaffected by them. In this world, nothing is everlasting. Time changes everything.

Practical Example:

Imagine a young student named Aman who is preparing for a crucial competitive exam. He is facing immense pressure and stress due to the high expectations of his family and society. He is constantly worried about his performance and is experiencing a rollercoaster of emotions, including anxiety and frustration. In this situation, Shloka 2.14 becomes highly relevant for Aman.

Transient Nature of Experiences: The verse reminds Aman that the sensations and experiences he is going through—whether it's the stress of studying, the fear of failure, or the moments of success—are transient. They come and go, just like the changing weather. Understanding that these experiences are impermanent can help him maintain emotional balance.

Pleasure and Pain: Aman may experience moments of pleasure when he makes progress in his studies and moments of pain when he faces challenges or setbacks. Shloka 2.14 advises him not to be overly attached to these fleeting experiences and to recognize that they are part of life's natural fluctuations.

Patience and Resilience: The verse encourages Aman to cultivate patience and resilience in the face of adversity. Instead of becoming overwhelmed by the highs and lows of his journey, he can practice tithiksha (endurance) and remain steadfast in his efforts.

Focus on the Goal: Aman's ultimate goal is to succeed in his exam. By keeping his focus on the bigger picture and the long-term objective, he can endure the temporary discomforts and distractions along the way.

In this way, Shloka 2.14 provides Aman with valuable guidance on how to navigate the challenges of his youth. It encourages him to maintain equanimity, remain patient during difficult times, and stay committed to his goals, understanding that the various sensations and experiences he encounters are transient and part of life's natural course. This wisdom can help him lead a more balanced and purposeful life as a young person.

हतो वा प्राप्स्यसि स्वर्गं जित्वा वा भोक्ष्यसे महीम्।तस्मादुत्तिष्ठ कौन्तेय युद्धाय कृतनिश्चयः ।।2.37।।

Meaning: Die, and you will win heaven; conquer, and you will enjoy sovereignty of the earth; therefore, stand up Arjuna, determined to fight.

Interpretation: Those who fight for the right cause enjoy the fruits of their victory. Initially, the struggle can be painful but the results are sweet. Let us take the example of a soldier who fights to safeguard the honor of the motherland and the safety of the people of the country. Even if he dies and his mortal remains come back draped in the national flag, he is remembered for his deeds of valor, and supreme sacrifice. Can there be a more glorious death?

This verse addresses Arjuna's dilemma about participating in the battle of Kurukshetra. It has broader implications for students, particularly in the context of making choices and pursuing their goals.

Facing Choices and Challenges: The verse acknowledges that life is filled with choices and challenges. Students, too, face various choices in their academic, personal, and career pursuits. These choices can be like a battlefield, where they must decide their path.

Embracing Determination: The verse encourages students to approach their goals with determination and resolve, much like Arjuna is urged to rise with determination for battle. This determination is essential for success, whether it's in academics, sports, arts, or any other endeavor.

Example: Consider Sarah, a high school student passionate about mathematics. She has the opportunity to participate in a prestigious mathematics competition. However, she's facing doubts and anxiety about the challenging problems and the possibility of not performing well.

In this situation, Shloka 2.37 can be applied:

Facing the Challenge: The verse reminds Sarah that life often presents choices and challenges. In her case, the mathematics competition is a challenge that could lead to a rewarding experience if she performs well (conquering the earth) or a valuable learning experience even if she doesn't perform as expected (attaining heaven).

Determination and Effort: Sarah can choose to approach this competition with determination, dedicating herself to preparation and giving her best effort. This attitude aligns with the verse's advice to "arise with determination."

Outcome Acceptance: The verse implies that the outcome may not always be what we expect, but our effort and determination are in our control. Whether she wins or loses the competition, Sarah can find growth and learning in the process.

In conclusion, Shloka 2.37 encourages students like Sarah to face life's challenges with determination and effort, knowing that the journey itself can be enriching and rewarding, regardless of the outcome. It encourages them to make choices and take actions that align with their goals and values.

सुखदुःखे समे कृत्वा लाभालाभौ जयाजयौ। ततो युद्धाय युज्यस्व नैवं पापमवाप्स्यसि॥ 2-38

Meaning: Holding pleasure and pain, gain and loss, victory, and defeat as alike, gird yourself up for the battle.

Interpretation: Maintain balance in life. The journey of life is like the journey of a river. We have rough patches and smooth passages. We have bumps but we have to move on like a river, honestly doing our duty. This verse imparts valuable wisdom about maintaining equanimity and a balanced perspective in the face of life's ups and downs. It advises youth to approach their endeavors with resilience and a sense of detachment from the outcomes.

Balanced Perspective: The verse suggests that youth should not be overly swayed by the dualities of life, such as pleasure and pain, gain and loss, or success and failure. Instead, they should strive to maintain a balanced and even-minded approach to these experiences.

Detachment from Outcomes: It encourages youth to detach themselves from the attachment to specific outcomes. Often, the fear of failure or the excessive desire for success can lead to stress and anxiety. By treating both victory and defeat alike, youth can free themselves from this mental burden.

Example: Let's consider the example of Maya, a young athlete who has trained rigorously for a national-level sports competition. The competition is highly competitive, and Maya is aiming for victory. However, as the competition progresses, she faces a challenging opponent and begins to feel immense pressure. In this context, Shloka 2.38 can be applied:

Balanced Approach: The verse advises Maya to treat both victory and defeat alike. Instead of being overwhelmed by the pressure to win, she can remind herself that winning is a goal, but it's not the sole measure of her worth or her effort.

Detachment from Outcomes: Maya can approach the competition with a mindset that focuses on giving her best effort and enjoying the process rather than being fixated solely on winning. She understands that her performance is under her control, but the outcome may not always be.

Resilience and Sportsmanship: Whether Maya wins or faces defeat, she can maintain her resilience and sportsmanship. By embracing both outcomes with equanimity, she can continue to grow as an athlete and as an individual.

In conclusion, Shloka 2.38 offers youth like Maya a practical approach to dealing with the challenges and uncertainties of life. It encourages them to maintain balance, detach from outcomes, and focus on their efforts and growth. This mindset can help youth navigate the various aspects of their lives with greater resilience and inner peace.

व्यवसायात्मिका बुद्धिरेकेह कुरुनन्दन। बहुशाखा ह्यनन्ताश्च बुद्धयोऽव्यवसायिनाम्।।2.41।।

Meaning Arjuna! There is only one faith and thought for those who practice this Karma Yoga. The minds of others are divided into various branches, and their thoughts and speculations are endless.

Interpretation: Be Focused. The various rays that pass through the concave lens of the sun become one and the heat generated by it can burn anything. If the rays are separated, they do not have the same power. Similarly, when your mind is focused, it gets immense power. Therefore, you need to collect your mind and bring your mind to the focal point. However, this can only be done if you are not attracted by all the things in the world that you want to have and enjoy. As long as you are attracted to all the worldly things, you will never have peace. Therefore, the only way to get peace is to focus and practice Karma yoga.

Students should remain focused and do extensive research into the field of study they are interested in. Once they have made up their minds, they should hold on to that decision. Repeatedly changing your mind and direction would lead to a series of fruitless, half-hearted attempts with no results. Plus, you might end up in a career that is not right for you.

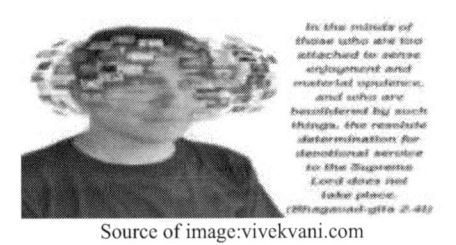

Source of image:vivekvani.com

कर्मण्येवाधिकारस्ते मा फलेषु कदाचन। मा कर्मफलहेतुर्भूर्मा ते सङ्गोऽस्त्वकर्मणि॥ 2-47

Meaning: You have a right to perform your prescribed duties, but you are not entitled to the fruits of your actions. Never consider yourself to be the cause of the results of your activities, nor be attached to inaction.

Interpretation: This is probably one of the most famous shlokas from the Bhagavad Gita. This emphasizes being process-oriented rather than result-oriented. Do your duty in the best possible manner and be detached from its outcome, do not get driven by the result, and enjoy the journey of reaching there. Because if the results do not turn around as per your expectations, pain is unavoidable. Work or action done with a constant expectation of rewards results in anxiety, restlessness, greed, dissatisfaction, etc. Whereas, something done without focusing on the rewards puts one in a positive frame. We are more focused when we concentrate on the work in our hands not the rewards of work.

This verse offers valuable guidance on the philosophy of detached action, emphasizing the importance of performing one's duties without attachment to the outcomes. Let's explore its relevance for students and professionals through examples.

For Students: Imagine a student named Rhea who is preparing for a critical examination. Her goal is to excel in the test, but she is also anxious about the results. Here's how Shloka 2.47 applies to her:

Prescribed Duties: Rhea's prescribed duty is to study diligently and prepare to the best of her ability. This is within her control, and she should focus on performing these duties effectively.

Detachment from Outcomes: The verse encourages Rhea not to fixate on the results (the fruits of her actions). While she can influence her preparation, she cannot entirely control the outcome of the examination. By detaching herself from the result, she can reduce anxiety and focus on her study without fear of failure.

Non-Attachment to Success or Failure: Rhea should not consider herself solely responsible for the result. Success or failure can depend on various factors, including external circumstances. By understanding this, she can maintain her peace of mind and avoid being overly distraught if the outcome is not as expected.

For Professionals: Consider a professional named Alex, who is working on a crucial project at the office. The success of the project could lead to a promotion. Here's how Shloka 2.47 applies to Alex:

Prescribed Duties: Alex's prescribed duty is to work diligently and contribute to the project to the best of his ability. He should focus on performing these duties effectively and professionally.

Detachment from Outcomes: The verse encourages Alex not to be overly attached to the promotion (the fruit of his actions). While he can influence the project's success, he cannot control the decision-making process entirely. Detaching from the outcome helps him maintain focus and reduce unnecessary stress.

Non-Attachment to Success or Failure: Alex should understand that his promotion may depend on various factors, including the decisions of others. By not considering himself solely responsible for the result, he can stay grounded and composed, even if the promotion doesn't materialize as expected.

In conclusion, Shloka 2.47 advises both students and professionals to perform their duties diligently and professionally but to detach themselves from the outcomes. This philosophy can lead to greater peace of mind, reduced anxiety, and a focus on the quality of their efforts rather than being solely results-driven.

क्रोधान्द्भवति सम्मोहः सम्मोहात्स्मृतिविभ्रमः।स्मृतिभ्रंशाद् बुद्धिनाशो बुद्धिनाशात्प्रणश्यति॥
2-63

Meaning: Anger clouds judgment, resulting in memory confusion. When the memory is confused, the intellect is destroyed; and when the intellect is destroyed, one is wrecked .
Interpretation: When someone is angry, he loses the ability to evaluate what is right and wrong. As a result, he weakens the strength of his mind, and as it is stated, a person cannot do anything in life without intellect. He's doomed. The rapid explosion of fury creates mental confusion and undermines the ability to analyze and judge.

Explanation with a Day-to-Day Life Example: Imagine a scenario in which a person experiences the destructive consequences of allowing anger to take control.

1. **Anger**: Let's say a person is stuck in a traffic jam on his way to an important meeting. He becomes increasingly frustrated and angry due to the delay caused by the traffic.

2. **Delusion**: As his anger intensifies, he starts to lose perspective and judgment. He might begin to think irrationally and emotionally. In this state of anger, he might believe that the entire world is conspiring

against him or that every driver on the road is intentionally causing the traffic jam.

3. **Confused Memory**: His delusion leads to confusion in his memory. He may recall past experiences of traffic jams or delays in a distorted and exaggerated manner, reinforcing his negative emotions.

4. **Ruin of Reason**: As his memory becomes increasingly distorted and his emotions cloud his judgment, his ability to think rationally and make informed decisions diminishes. He might make impulsive decisions like taking reckless shortcuts or getting into unnecessary arguments with other drivers.

5. **Perishing**: Ultimately, if he allows anger to persist and take control, it can lead to disastrous consequences. He might make a reckless move on the road that results in an accident, putting his safety and the safety of others at risk. This represents the "perishing" mentioned in the verse, which can have severe real-life consequences.

In this day-to-day life example, the verse illustrates how unchecked anger can lead to a chain of negative consequences, starting from delusion and culminating in the loss of rational thinking and potentially harmful actions. It serves as a cautionary lesson about the importance of managing anger and maintaining emotional control to make wise decisions and avoid unnecessary harm in one's life.

आपूर्यमाणमचलप्रतिष्ठं समुद्रमापः प्रविशन्ति यद्वत् ।तद्वत्कामा यं प्रविशन्ति सर्वेस शान्तिमाप्नोति न कामकामी ॥ 2.70

Meaning: Just as the ocean remains undisturbed by the incessant flow of waters from rivers merging into it, likewise the sage who is unmoved despite the flow of desirable objects all around him attains peace, and not the person who strives to satisfy desires.

Interpretation: Numerous streams of water enter a deep, wide ocean. No matter how many streams there are in the ocean, or how strongly or gently they enter it, the ocean is always quiet and undisturbed. Similarly, a person with a stable understanding has all of these "thoughts, needs, expectations, and desires" (rivers) flowing in the mind (ocean), yet he or she is unaffected by and unbothered by them. No matter how many material possessions or desires he or she has, the person is unaffected. Learn to control desires like Yogi. Student life is a period of penance. Indulging in too much pleasure will obstruct your concentration. You will always remain distracted. Let's explore its relevance for both youth and professionals.

For Youth: Imagine a young person named Aisha who is in high school. She's ambitious and wants to excel academically. However, she also faces peer pressure to fit in, have a busy social life, and indulges in various extracurricular activities. Here's how Shloka 2.70 applies to Aisha:

The Ocean of Equanimity: The verse compares the mind to an ocean that remains ever full and undisturbed. Aisha should strive to cultivate a calm and composed mind, like the unruffled surface of the ocean.

Influx of Desires: Just as waters naturally flow into the ocean, desires will naturally arise in Aisha's heart. These desires may include the pursuit of academic success, social recognition, or personal interests.

Maintaining Inner Peace: The verse suggests that Aisha should remain tranquil and undisturbed by these desires. She can prioritize her goals, manage her time effectively, and make choices that align with her values without succumbing to external pressures or conflicting desires.

Achieving Peace without Being Overly Ambitious: Aisha can work towards her academic and personal goals without becoming overly ambitious or losing her inner peace. The realization that contentment doesn't come from constantly pursuing desires can guide her choices.

For Professionals: Consider a professional named Raj who is working in a high-pressure corporate job. He has career aspirations, but he also faces the demands of the job, competition, and the desire for work-life balance. Here's how Shloka 2.70 applies to Raj.

The Ocean of Equanimity: The verse encourages Raj to maintain a sense of inner calm and steadiness amidst the busyness and demands of his professional life.

Influx of Desires: Like the flowing waters, Raj experiences various desires related to career growth, recognition, financial stability, and personal fulfillment.

Maintaining Inner Peace: Raj should strive to manage his desires without letting them disturb his inner peace. He can set clear priorities, establish boundaries, and make choices that align with his long-term well-being and values.

Achieving Peace without Becoming Overly Ambitious: Raj can work towards his professional goals without becoming overly ambitious or neglecting his personal life. This balance will enable him to achieve success without sacrificing his peace of mind.

In summary, Shloka 2.70 offers guidance to both youth and professionals on how to maintain inner peace and composure while navigating the influx of desires and external pressures. It encourages them to prioritize their goals and make choices in alignment with their values, leading to a more balanced and fulfilling life.

योगस्थः कुरु कर्माणि सङ्गं त्यक्त्वा धनञ्जय।सिद्ध्यसिद्ध्योः समो भूत्वा समत्वं योग उच्यते॥ 2-48

Meaning: By being established in Yoga, O Dhananjaya, undertake actions, casting off attachment and remaining equipoised in success and failure. Equanimity is called Yoga.

Interpretation: Karma Yoga is defined as doing one's duty while maintaining equanimity under all circumstances. Pain and pleasure, birth and death, loss and gain, union and separation are inevitable, being under the control of one's past deeds or Karma, like the coming of day and night. Fools rejoice in prosperity and mourn in adversity, but a Karma Yogi remains tranquil under all circumstances. (VivekaVani, https://vivekavani.com/b2v48/)Let's explore how this advice applies to both youth and professionals.

For Youth: Imagine a young person named Rahul who is preparing for a sports competition. He is passionate about winning and representing his school. However, he also faces the fear of failure and the pressure to meet expectations. Here's how Shloka 2.48 applies to Rahul.

Performing Duties Equipoised: The verse suggests that Rahul should put in his best effort and dedication into his training and competition, regardless of whether he wins or loses.

Abandoning Attachment to Success or Failure: Rahul should detach himself from the attachment to winning or losing. He should understand that while winning is a goal, it doesn't define his worth or effort.

Maintaining Equanimity: By practicing equanimity, Rahul can face the competition with a calm and balanced mindset. This will help him perform better under pressure and reduce anxiety.

Embracing the Learning Process: Regardless of the outcome, Rahul can see every competition as an opportunity for growth and learning. This perspective allows him to improve continuously.

For Professionals: Consider a professional named Amrita who is leading a high-stakes project at her company. She is ambitious and wants the project to succeed, but she also faces challenges and uncertainties. Here's how Shloka 2.48 applies to Amrita:

Performing Duties Equipoised: Amrita should focus on managing the project with diligence, competence, and dedication, regardless of whether it meets all its goals or faces setbacks.

Abandoning Attachment to Success or Failure: Amrita should detach herself from the obsession with project success. She can acknowledge that there are external factors and variables beyond her control.

Maintaining Equanimity: By practicing equanimity, Amrita can lead her team with a calm and balanced approach, even during challenging phases of the project. This can improve team morale and efficiency.

Embracing Continuous Improvement: Regardless of the project's final outcome, Amrita can see it as an opportunity for learning and refinement of her leadership and project management skills.

In summary, Shloka 2.48 advises youth like Rahul and professionals like Amrita to focus on their duties and responsibilities with dedication and detachment from the results. It encourages them to maintain equanimity, reduce stress, and find growth and learning in their pursuits, ultimately leading to a more balanced and fulfilling life or career.

यदा संहरते चायं कूर्मोऽङ्गानीव सर्वशः।

इन्द्रियाणीन्द्रियार्थेभ्यस्तस्य प्रज्ञा प्रतिष्ठिता ॥2. 58॥

Meaning: One who is able to withdraw the senses from their objects, just as a tortoise withdraws its limbs into its shell, is established in divine wisdom

Interpretation: For yogis and students, this shloka is important. Control over the senses is crucial for achieving self-realization. It implies that the mind should be focused on the objective, goal rather than the senses, which by nature want to chase after external objects. One's understanding becomes flawless when this is done firmly and there is no deviation from the goal. An image and an example are used to bring out this concept very clearly.

When the tortoise perceives even the slightest threat from the outside, it immediately retracts all of its limbs into its shell. Even if the shell were torn to bits, its limbs would not stretch. Like a tortoise, a yogi or student should withdraw their senses from the outside world and center themselves within. The yogi should shut off all of his senses to anything in the outside world. Even though all doors are locked except one, a robber can still enter the house through the unlocked one. A burst of wind from one window, even if it is left open, could put out the lamp. Therefore, if you want to achieve your aim, all of your senses must be under control. You'll be distracted by overeating, oversleeping, procrastination, and engaging in excessively enjoyable hobbies. Thus, the most important spiritual discipline is sense control.

Example: Imagine a student named Meera who is preparing for important exams. She is constantly distracted by her smartphone, social media, and other leisure activities. Here's how Shloka 2.58 applies to Meera:

Withdrawal of Senses: The verse suggests that Meera should exercise self-control by withdrawing her senses from distractions. She can create a dedicated study environment free from temptations like her phone and social media.

Focusing on Studies: By practicing this self-control, Meera can fully focus on her studies. This will improve her concentration, retention of information, and ultimately, her academic performance.

Steady Wisdom: With steady and focused study habits, Meera's wisdom in the subject matter she is studying will grow steadily. She will become more adept at grasping concepts and applying them effectively in exams.

Achieving Academic Success: Meera 's dedication to her studies, with a clear mind free from distractions, will enhance her academic achievements and set her up for success.

For Professionals: Consider a professional named Raman who works in a fast-paced corporate environment. He often finds himself multitasking, constantly checking emails, and attending numerous meetings. Here's how Shloka 2.58 applies to Raman:

Withdrawal of Senses from Distractions: The verse advises Raman to exercise self-control by withdrawing his senses from distractions like constant email checking or over-participating in meetings.

Focused Work: By practicing this self-control, Raman can prioritize his tasks, allocate dedicated time for focused work, and avoid multitasking. This can lead to improved productivity and better-quality output.

Steady Wisdom in Decision-Making: With a clear and focused mind, Raman 's wisdom in making critical decisions for his projects or team will become steadier. He can think more clearly and make well-informed choices.

Professional Growth: Raman's disciplined approach to work and decision-making will contribute to his professional growth, leadership skills, and ability to handle challenging situations effectively.

In summary, Shloka 2.58 advises both students and professionals to practice self-control by withdrawing their senses from distractions and focusing on their respective responsibilities. This disciplined approach leads to a steady and improved wisdom, ultimately contributing to their success in academics or their professional endeavors.

नास्ति बुद्धिरयुक्तस्य न चायुक्तस्य भावना। न चाभावयतः शान्तिरशान्तस्य कुतः सुखम्॥
2-66

Meaning: For the unsteady, there is no wisdom, and there is no meditation for the unsteady man. And for an un-meditated man, there is no peace. How can there be happiness for one without peace?

Interpretation: This verse highlights the importance of having a calm and controlled mind. It says that someone who lacks proper understanding, clear thinking, and control over his mind cannot find true happiness or peace.

For students, this implies that effective learning and understanding require concentration. Without a focused and connected mind, it's challenging to grasp and retain knowledge. A distracted student may struggle to comprehend the subject. If students are not mentally present and focused on their studies, they may not perform well academically, which can lead to stress and unhappiness. Imagine a student who is constantly checking his phone, chatting with friends, or watching TV while trying to study for an important exam. He is not connected or focused on his studies. As a result, he may struggle to understand the material, perform poorly in exams, and feel stressed about his grades.

For professionals, being connected means being fully engaged in your work or tasks. If you're constantly distracted or not fully present at your job, your productivity and quality of work can suffer. Consider a professional in a corporate setting who attends meetings but spends most of the time thinking about personal matters or browsing the internet. This lack of connection to the work at hand can lead to missed opportunities, decreased productivity, and a lack of job satisfaction.

The verse encourages individuals to cultivate focus, mindfulness, and dedication in their pursuits, whether it's studying or working professionally.

यद्यदाचरति श्रेष्ठस्तत्तदेवेतरो जनः। स यत्प्रमाणं कुरुते लोकस्तदनुवर्तते।।3.21।।

Meaning: Whatever a superior person does, another person does that very thing! Whatever he upholds as an authority, an ordinary person follows that.

Interpretation: The Lord argues the issue from a practical point of view. The common people watch the behaviour of prominent men who hold impressive positions in the world. Naturally, they behave in the same manner. Children copy what adults do. We witness this constantly and very frequently: people use the lives of great men as examples for justifying their own behaviour. As a result, a man should exercise extraordinary caution as he assumes leadership and assumes a prominent role. That man has a responsibility to maintain a high standard of moral and spiritual behaviour.

Whatever action a great man performs, common men follow. And whatever standards he sets by exemplary acts, all the world pursues.
Bhagavad-gita 3.21

Consider a professional in a corporate setting who consistently demonstrates ethical conduct, teamwork, and dedication to his work. He treats colleagues with respect, is punctual for meetings, and always strives for excellence. Colleagues and subordinates observe and are influenced by this professional's behaviour. They, too, start adhering to ethical standards, collaborating effectively, and showing commitment to their work. The professional's example sets a high standard for professionalism and ethics in the workplace, leading to a more harmonious and productive work environment.

श्रेयान्स्वधर्मो विगुणः परधर्मात्स्वनुष्ठितात्। स्वधर्मे निधनं श्रेयः परधर्मो भयावहः।।3.35।।

Meaning: One's own duty, though devoid of merit, is preferable to the duty of another well performed. Even death in the performance of one's own duty brings blessedness; another's duty is fraught with fear.

Interpretation: Being a Kshatriya, Arjuna was duty bound to fight righteous war. Arjuna expressed his sorrow by saying that he would rather live off on alms like a poor person than slaughter his family and friends in battle. Here, the Lord explains the rules for Kshatriyas and the risks associated with disobeying them and living someone else's life.is. He must wage a just battle, even though doing so could result in his demise. It is risky to abandon one's duty and take on another person's, as this would upset the natural order of things and lead to anarchy and confusion in society.

Consider a professional who is highly skilled in marketing but is asked to take on a managerial role for which he has no interest or aptitude. Despite his expertise in marketing, he accepts the managerial role because it comes with a higher salary. What would be the result? The professional would struggle to manage teams effectively, leading to decreased morale and productivity. By not following his true calling, he might find himself stressed, unfulfilled, and facing career burnout. The verse advises individuals to prioritize their own dharma or true calling.

इन्द्रियाणि पराण्याहुरिन्द्रियेभ्यः परं मनः । मनसस्तु परा बुद्धिर्यो बुद्धेः परतस्तु सः ॥3-42

Meaning: The senses are superior to the gross body and superior to the senses is the mind. Beyond the mind is the intellect, and even beyond the intellect is the soul.

Interpretation: Our Atma, our conscience always guides us to be on the right path. This verse talks about the hierarchy of our inner faculties.

Indriyas (Senses): The verse begins by saying that our senses (like eyes, ears, nose, etc.) are inferior to the mind. It means that our senses alone cannot make decisions or understand things on their own.

Mind: It then says that the mind is superior to the senses. This means that the mind controls and processes the information received from the senses. It's like the boss that makes decisions based on what the senses perceive.

Buddhi (Intellect): Next, it says that the intellect (or intelligence) is even higher than the mind. The intellect is responsible for analyzing and making wise judgments. It's like the manager who guides the mind in making decisions.

Atman (Soul or True Self): Finally, it mentions something beyond the intellect, which is often referred to as the true self or soul. This higher aspect is beyond our intellect and represents our deepest and most divine nature.

So, in simple terms, this verse emphasizes that there is a hierarchy within us: Senses < Mind < Intellect < True Self. It suggests that we should strive to go beyond the senses and even the intellect to connect with our true and higher self and make right decisions.

उद्धरेदात्मनाऽऽत्मानंनात्मानमवसादयेत्।आत्मैव ह्यात्मनो बन्धुरात्मैव रिपुरात्मनः।।6.5।।

Meaning: Elevate yourself through your own efforts, and not degrade yourself. For, the mind can be the friend and also the enemy of the self.

Interpretation: This verse suggests that a person has the power to elevate himself or degrade himself based on his own actions and thoughts. One's mind can be his best friend or worst enemy, depending on how it is managed. Imagine a student facing a challenging academic situation, such as preparing for a tough examination.

Friendship with the Self: If the student practices self-discipline, sets a structured study schedule, and maintains a positive mindset, he can excel in his studies. In this scenario, his own self (mind) becomes a friend by helping him achieve his academic goals.

Enmity with the Self: On the contrary, if the student procrastinates, becomes distracted easily, or engages in self-doubt and negative thinking, his own self (mind) can become his enemy. These self-sabotaging behaviours may lead to poor academic performance and emotional distress.

This verse encourages us to uplift ourselves through self-discipline and positive thinking, turning our own minds into a friend rather than an enemy. By mastering our own minds and making choices that are conducive to our goals of life and well-being, we can elevate ourselves and lead more fulfilling lives.

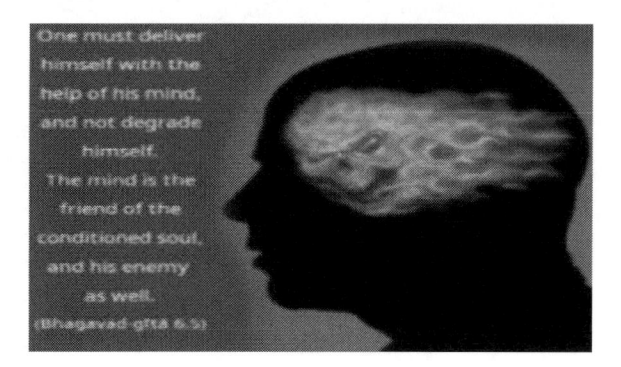

> One must deliver himself with the help of his mind, and not degrade himself. The mind is the friend of the conditioned soul, and his enemy as well.
> (Bhagavad-gītā 6.5)

बन्धुरात्मात्मनस्तस्य येनात्मैवात्मना जितः। अनात्मनस्तु शत्रुत्वे स्थितप्रज्ञस्तदोच्यते पार्थ सः ॥6.6

Meaning: For him who has conquered the mind, the mind is the best of friends; but for one who has failed to do so, his very mind will be the greatest enemy.

Interpretation: This verse speaks about the importance of mastering the mind. It suggests that when we are able to control and discipline our own thoughts, our mind becomes a trusted ally, guiding us towards peace and inner strength. On the other hand, if we allow our mind to wander unchecked, it can become a source of distraction and turmoil, leading us away from our goals and causing inner conflict. By understanding this teaching, we can strive to cultivate mental discipline and harness the power of our mind to support our well-being and spiritual growth.

Example: Let's consider a real-life example to illustrate the concept from Chapter 6, Verse 6 of the Bhagavad Gita. Imagine you have a big presentation at work coming up, and you're feeling quite nervous about it. Your mind starts racing with thoughts of self-doubt and worry. You begin to imagine all the things that could go wrong, causing anxiety and making it difficult to focus on preparing for the presentation. In this scenario, if you have mastered your mind, you would be able to recognize these negative thoughts and emotions, and consciously redirect your focus towards positive and productive thinking. You would remind yourself of your capabilities, visualize a successful outcome, and take practical steps to prepare with confidence. In doing so, your mind becomes a supportive friend, helping you stay focused, calm, and motivated throughout the process.

On the other hand, if you haven't yet gained mastery over your mind, negative thoughts may persistently dominate your thinking. You might find yourself dwelling on worst-case scenarios, continuously imagining the most unfavorable outcomes. As a result, you may become overwhelmed by anxiety and struggle to maintain focus on your preparations. In this scenario, your mind transforms into an adversary, obstructing your progress and intensifying your stress.

By understanding the importance of controlling our thoughts and emotions, we can strive to cultivate a positive and focused mindset, turning our mind into a valuable ally in navigating life's challenges.

युक्ताहारविहारस्य युक्तचेष्टस्य कर्मसु। युक्तस्वप्नावबोधस्य योगो भवति दु:खहा।।6.17।।

Meaning: Those who are disciplined in eating and recreation, balanced in work, and regulated in sleep, can mitigate all sorrows by practicing Yoga.

Interpretation: The Lord says, "Be moderate, avoid excess in all things.". Therefore, if a man experiences suffering, excessive indulgence of some kind is to blame. In reality, self-control refers to a person's ability to command his body and mind to behave in accordance with the highest spiritual rules. For the man whose body and intellect function independently of the spiritual principles, there is no self-control. Overindulgence can be just as damaging as underindulgence. Young students stay up late studying for exams, but when it comes time to write them, they are too worn out and their preparation goes in vain. Even if they succeed in the test, the aftereffects of overwork result in one disease or another. **In actuality, harmony, balance, and moderation are the principles**

upon which the body itself is created and maintained. It burns in excess heat, and it stiffens in excess cold. The eyes cannot see in excessive light, yet they cannot see in complete darkness either. Extremes are alike. The body needs a moderate amount of warmth and light to function properly. The analogy might likewise be applied to the mind also. Overstudying dulls the mind, leads to exhaustion, and aggravates nervous disorders. Emotional excess leads to insanity. Intense mental conflict and stress cause the nervous system to malfunction. **Therefore, harmony and balance are essential to human existence. It is the law of nature.**

त्रिविधं नरकस्येदं द्वारं नाशनमात्मन: |काम: क्रोधस्तथा लोभस्तस्मादेतत्त्रयं त्यजेत् ||16.21||

Meaning: Lust, anger, and greed are the three gates that lead to the inferno of self-destruction for the soul. As a result, everyone should abandon these three.

Interpretation: In this verse, Lord Krishna is teaching Arjuna about the three gates that lead to self-destructive behavior and ultimately to hell. These gates are desire, anger, and greed, and the verse advises one to renounce these qualities to attain spiritual growth and liberation. Let us understand each of these gates with practical examples.

Desire: Desire refers to an insatiable craving or longing for things or experiences that are often materialistic or sensual in nature. When desire is unchecked, it can lead to attachment and suffering.

Material Possessions: Constantly desiring more and more material possessions, such as expensive cars, designer clothing, or the latest gadgets, can lead to discontent and financial stress.

Sensual Pleasures: Excessive indulgence in sensual pleasures like food, alcohol, or sexual desires can lead to physical and emotional harm.

Anger: Anger is an intense emotional response to a perceived provocation, injustice, or frustration. Uncontrolled anger can harm relationships and one's own well-being. Practical examples of anger include:

Road Rage: Getting excessively angry and aggressive while driving due to traffic or other drivers' behaviour can lead to dangerous situations and accidents.

Conflict in Relationships: Frequent outbursts of anger in personal relationships can damage trust and lead to emotional turmoil.

Greed: Greed is an excessive desire for wealth, possessions, or power. It can lead to unethical behavior and disregard for the well-being of others. Practical examples of greed include:

Financial Fraud: Individuals driven by greed may engage in fraudulent activities to amass wealth at the expense of others.

Hoarding Wealth: Accumulating vast wealth without using it for charitable or meaningful purposes can be seen as greed, as it perpetuates inequality and suffering.

The verse advises renouncing these three qualities as they can lead to a life of suffering and spiritual stagnation. By cultivating qualities like contentment, compassion, and self-control, individuals can progress on the path of spiritual growth and liberation.

"These evils lurking in the heart like thieves in darkness should be

detected by the torchlight of knowledge and should be driven out with the help of the Divine qualities." Vivekananda

HOW LUST, ANGER & GREED MAKE OUR LIFE HELLISH

असंशयं महाबाहो मनो दुर्निग्रहं चलं। अभ्यासेन तु कौन्तेय वैराग्येण च गृह्यते।। 6-35

Meaning: O mighty-armed son of Kunti, it is undoubtedly tough to curb the restless mind, but it is possible by constant practice and detachment.

Interpretation: The Lord acknowledges that because the mind is restless, it is very difficult to restrain it. However, there is no need to give up. Practice and objectivity are necessary for control. The greatest teacher emphasizes that there are strategies for getting over the obstacles of mind control. While acknowledging Arjuna's restless mind, the Lord reassures him that there is a way to regulate it, and that method is via practice and dispassion. If one is equipped with a stronger weapon than the enemy, one need not be afraid of his power. Even if the elephant is powerful, holding the iron rod is sufficient. Let us take the example of a professional facing a demanding and stressful project at work.

Restless Mind: The professional's mind is constantly filled with worries, stress, and anxieties related to work deadlines and responsibilities. This mental agitation affects his performance and well-being.

Practice: The professional starts practicing mindfulness and stress reduction techniques. This includes regular meditation and breathing exercises to calm the mind and bring it back to the present moment.

Detachment: The professional practices detachment by setting boundaries for work-related concerns. He avoids constantly checking emails or thinking about work during his personal time.

Result: Through consistent practice and detachment from work-related worries, the professional manages to reduce stress and increase his ability to focus on tasks. This results in improved productivity and a better work-life balance. The verse teaches that while the mind is naturally restless and hard to control, it can be tamed through practice and detachment. Students and professionals can use these principles to improve their ability to concentrate, reduce stress, and enhance their performance in their respective endeavours.

दातव्यमिति यद्दानं दीयतेऽनुपकारिणे। देशे काले च पात्रे च तद्दानं सात्त्विकं स्मृतम्।।17.20।

Meaning: Charity given to a worthy person simply because it is right to give, without consideration of anything in return, at the proper time and in the proper place, is stated to be in the mode of goodness.

Interpretation: Every man should perform acts of generosity as a sacred responsibility, not for the purpose of acquiring respect or reputation in society. The motivation behind any act of kindness should be "It is my duty to offer this gift to this man, and therefore I am giving it". In actuality, whatever sacrifice we make for the sake of others, is a good done unto one's own self .Therefore, when we help the poor and those in need, let us keep in mind that we are not providing for them because the Lord provides for all of us, but rather we are building to the mountain of our own righteousness, which will significantly further our own spiritual goal.

Charity offered to persons from whom no return benefit is expected, is the highest. Charity should be given to the truly needy, the blind, the lame, the ill, and the abandoned. It is done out of pure compassion, and such sentiments soften the heart and enable individuals realize the truth of the oneness of all beings. Gifts given to the wealthy and powerful are tainted by the secret intention of receiving benefits from them in due time. As a result, it is not a deed of spiritual merit.

For Students: Imagine a student who wants to help a classmate struggling with his studies.

Giving with No Expectation: The student offers help to his classmate without expecting anything in return, such as repayment or favors in the future. This aligns with the idea of giving without any expectation of personal gain.

Proper Place and Time: The student offers his assistance in an appropriate setting, like during study sessions or after class, ensuring it doesn't disrupt other activities. He also provides help when his classmate genuinely needs it.

Worthy Recipient: The student helps a sincere classmate who genuinely seeks to improve his academic performance and is putting an effort. He avoids aiding someone who is simply looking for shortcuts or not making an honest effort.

Result: By offering help without any expectation of personal gain, in the right place and time, and to a deserving classmate, the student's act of charity is considered virtuous. It promotes a culture of mutual support and cooperation among students.

For Professionals: Consider a professional in a corporate environment who wants to make a charitable donation.

Giving with No Expectation: The professional donates to a charitable cause or organization without expecting personal benefits or recognition in return. He is motivated by a genuine desire to contribute to a cause.

Proper Place and Time: The donation is made to a reputable charity or organization at a suitable time, aligning with their mission and goals. The donation does not disrupt the professional's work responsibilities.

Worthy Recipient: The donation is directed to a cause that genuinely helps those in need or advances a significant societal or environmental cause. It is not used for self-serving or unethical purposes.

Result: The professional's charitable donation, made without expecting personal gain, to a reputable and worthy cause, is considered virtuous. It demonstrates a commitment to social responsibility and ethical behavior in the corporate world.

In both student and professional scenarios, the verse underscores the importance of charitable giving characterized by selflessness, proper timing and place, and a genuine intention to help deserving recipients. Such acts of charity promote a sense of social responsibility and contribute positively to the community or workplace.

नियतं सङ्गरहितमरागद्वेषतः कृतम् फलप्रेप्सुना कर्म यतत्सात्त्विकमुच्यते॥18-23

Meaning: Ordained by the Shastras, that action, performed by one not desirous of the fruit, without attachment, free from love and hate, is called Sattvic karma

Interpretation: It is essential to understand the basic principles of action since no man can survive without it and because, as we can see, action is life itself.

1. Action should follow the Shastras' guidelines.

2. It should be carried out without attachments and without any sense of doer ship.

3. There should be no attraction or aversion.

4. It needs to be performed without desiring the fruit.

This verse highlights the qualities and intentions behind an action that make it sattvic (virtuous or in the mode of goodness).

Consider a professional working on a project with a sattvic approach:

Ordained Action: The professional approaches the project with a well-defined plan, clear objectives, and a structured workflow. He follows a systematic approach.

Free from Attachment: The professional works on the project without excessive attachment to personal glory or success. He understands that outcomes are influenced by various factors beyond his control.

Free from Love and Hatred: The professional treats all team members and aspects of the project with fairness and equanimity, without showing favouritism or harbouring grudges.

No Desire for Reward: The professional is motivated by a genuine passion for work, wanting to excel for the sake of personal growth and the satisfaction of contributing to the team and organization. He does not work solely for external rewards or recognition.

Result: In this context, the professional's approach to work reflects sattvic qualities. He carries out his responsibilities diligently, without attachment to personal gain, without favouritism or bias, and with a genuine desire for excellence. This often leads to improved teamwork, quality work, and professional growth.

The verse emphasizes the importance of performing actions with sattvic qualities, which include disciplined and focused efforts, detachment from outcomes, equanimity, and a genuine desire for self-improvement and the betterment of the project. Such actions tend to yield positive results and personal growth.

मुक्तसङ्गोऽनहंवादी धृत्युत्साहसमन्वितः ।सिद्ध्यसिद्ध्योर्निर्विकारः कर्ता सात्त्विक उच्यते ॥18- 26॥

Meaning: An actor agent who is freed from attachment, non-egotistic, unaffected in success and failure, endued with firmness and enthusiasm, is called Sattvic (Karta).

Interpretation: Nature of Satvic Agent-

1. He is unconcerned with the fruits of action;
2. He has abandoned the notion that he is the actor;
3. He is firm and enthusiastic in all work;
4. He is unaffected by success or failure."

This verse describes the characteristics of actions performed with a sattvic (virtuous) approach.

For Students: Imagine a student preparing for an exam with a sattvic approach:

Free from Attachments: The student studies with a mindset that is free from attachments to external rewards like grades or recognition. They are motivated by a genuine love for learning and personal growth rather than by the desire for external validation.

Without False Ego: The student does not boast about his knowledge or belittle others. He approaches his studies with humility and is open to learning from both successes and mistakes.

Resolute: The student maintains a steady and unwavering focus on his studies, regardless of distractions or challenges. He is determined to achieve his goals.

Enthusiastic: The student approaches his studies with enthusiasm and a positive attitude, finding joy in the process of learning.

Unaffected by Success or Failure : The student is not overly elated by success or demotivated by failure. He understands that both success and failure are part of the learning journey.

Result: In this scenario, the student's approach to studying is sattvic. His actions are driven by a genuine love for learning, humility, determination, enthusiasm, and an understanding that success and failure are part of the learning process. This approach often leads to not only academic success but also personal growth and a well-rounded education.

For Professionals: Consider a professional working on a project with a sattvic approach:

Free from Attachments: The professional is motivated by the desire to do his best work and contribute to the success of the project, rather than by personal gain or recognition.

Without False Ego: The professional works collaboratively with colleagues, acknowledging their contributions valuing teamwork. He does not wish to take credit for others' efforts.

Resolute: The professional remains committed to the project's objectives, even when faced with challenges or setbacks. He stays focused on achieving the project's goals.

Enthusiastic: The professional approaches his work with enthusiasm and a positive attitude, finding satisfaction in the process of contributing to the project's success.

Unaffected by Success or Failure: The professional remains balanced and composed, not getting overly elated by success or demotivated by temporary setbacks.

Result: In this context, the professional's approach to work is sattvic. His actions are driven by a genuine commitment to the project's success, humility, determination, enthusiasm, and an understanding that success and occasional setbacks are part of the professional journey. This approach often leads to effective teamwork and project success.

In both student and professional scenarios, the verse emphasizes that actions driven by a sattvic approach are characterized by qualities such as humility, determination, enthusiasm, and a focus on the process rather than the outcome. Such actions tend to result in personal and professional growth and contribute positively to the overall environment.

न हि देहभृता शक्यं त्यक्तुं कर्माण्यशेषतः |यस्तु कर्मफलत्यागी स त्यागीत्यभिधीयते ||18.11||

Meaning: It is difficult for the embodied entity to cease all actions. Those who give up the fruits of their acts, on the other hand, are said to be really renounced.

Interpretation: The renunciation of the benefits of activities is preferable to renunciation of all actions because there will be no distraction from meditation and contemplation. Shri Krishna dismisses this as a possibility, claiming that the human being cannot exist in a condition of utter inactivity. Everyone must execute the basic duties of physical care, such as eating, sleeping, bathing, and so on. Furthermore, standing, sitting, thinking, walking, chatting, and other activities cannot be avoided.

Even just maintaining the body requires the embodied being to take action. Anyone cannot completely give up taking action. As a result, the ideal way to live is to work without thinking about the benefits you might receive from doing so. The distinguishing quality of doing all the effort while being disinterested in the results is the characteristic feature of the true Tyagi.

यज्ञदानतपःकर्म न त्याज्यं कार्यमेव तत्। यज्ञो दानं तपश्चैव पावनानि मनीषिणाम्।।18.5।।

Meaning: Acts of sacrifice, charity, and austerity should not be abandoned; they should be performed indeed; sacrifice, charity, and austerity are purifiers for the thoughtful.

Interpretation: The Lord cautions us in this verse to continue practicing virtues like kindness, sacrifice, and austerity. He demands that they be carried out. Why is there any reason for uncertainty, and why should man degrade by disobeying the Lord's command? These virtuous deeds purify the mind and soul when they are carried out selflessly. Work, help, and care selflessly.

यदा यदा हि धर्मस्य ग्लानिर्भवति भारत ।अभ्युत्थानमधर्मस्य तदात्मानं सृजाम्यहम् ॥4-7॥
परित्राणाय साधूनां विनाशाय च दुष्कृताम् ।धर्मसंस्थापनार्थाय सम्भवामि युगे युगे ॥4-8॥

Meaning: Whenever there is decay of righteousness, O Bharata, and there is an exaltation of unrighteousness, then I come forth for the protection of the good, for the destruction of evil-doers, for the sake of firmly establishing righteousness, I am born from age to age.

Interpretation: This verse speaks about the cycle of dharma or righteousness in the world. It states that Lord Krishna is an incarnation of Lord Vishnu and whenever there is a decline in righteousness, he appears on earth to bring balance and harmony. This verse has a deeper spiritual significance. The verse suggests that each of us has a spark of divinity within us, which we can tap into to make the right choices in life whenever we face ethical dilemmas.

56. How Relevant Is the Bhagvad Gita in Today's World?

Everyone has an innate desire for happiness, regardless of their age, nationality, religion, or gender. However, in our relentless search for genuine happiness, many people are becoming increasingly disillusioned. But fear not! The Bhagavad Gita holds the key to unlocking true happiness and life satisfaction. Just like a user manual that accompanies every new gadget we buy; the Gita serves as a divine manual bestowed upon us by the Supreme Lord Krishna. It teaches us how to navigate through life and make the most of our human experience. In today's perplexing and misguided world, the significance of the Gita becomes even more pronounced. It has the power to restore stability and happiness in both individual lives and society as a whole. So, let's embrace the wisdom of the Bhagavad Gita and embark on a journey towards lasting happiness and fulfillment!

We have discussed a few shlokas from Shrimad Bhagwat Gita with meaning and interpretation. This great book is a mine of wisdom. Contrary to popular belief, the Gita is not exclusively meant for senior citizens or as a mere armchair read for the elderly. Its teachings hold immense value for the younger generation as well, as it provides invaluable guidance for navigating the journey of life with success and serenity. When you find yourself restless and things aren't going according to plan, studying the Shrimad Bhagwat Gita can bring you inner peace. In today's materialistic world, where values have taken a back seat and nature has been disrupted, it seems that the malevolent forces hold sway and humanity's very existence is threatened. However, in the face of these challenges, the profound dialogue between God and the human soul in the Gita can serve as a guiding light.

Let us embrace the timeless wisdom of the Shrimad Bhagwat Gita to find solace, restore harmony, and navigate the complexities of our modern world.

Epilogue: Taming the Monkey Mind

As we come to the end of our journey together, it is important to reflect on the lessons learned and the trans-formations experienced in taming the monkey mind. Throughout this book, we have explored various techniques and strategies to cultivate a sense of inner calm amid the chaos of our daily lives. But more importantly, we have discovered the profound importance of self-compassion, worldly wisdom, and spiritual orientation in this process.

Self-compassion has been at the heart of our endeavour to tame the monkey mind. We have learned to be gentle and kind to ourselves, embracing our imperfections and treating ourselves with the same love and understanding we extend to others. Through practicing self-compassion, we have discovered that the path towards inner peace begins with acceptance and forgiveness of ourselves.

In our exploration of worldly wisdom, we have recognized the significance of finding balance and equanimity in the face of life's numerous challenges. We have learned to navigate the ups and downs, understanding that everything is impermanent and that change is an inherent part of our existence. With this wisdom, we have gained clarity and resilience, enabling us to face the uncertainties of life with grace and undisturbed tranquillity.

However, we have also recognized that taming the monkey mind goes beyond just personal development. It encompasses a deeper spiritual journey that connects us to something greater than ourselves. While spiritual orientation may take different forms for each of us, it is the cultivation of our inner being, and the alignment of our thoughts, values, and actions with a higher purpose that brings a sense of profound fulfilment. Whether through meditation, prayer, or connecting with nature, we have found solace in nurturing our spiritual selves.

As we conclude this book, let us remember that taming the monkey mind is not a destination but a lifelong practice. It requires patience, commitment, and a willingness to cultivate self-awareness and inner growth. The monkey mind may resurface from time to time, but armed with the tools and understanding we have acquired, we are empowered to bring it back into alignment with our true selves.

May this journey serve as a reminder that within each of us lies the power to find stillness amidst the chaos, to embrace compassion for ourselves and others, to embody worldly wisdom, and to explore the depths of our spiritual orientation. May we continue to nourish and tame our monkey minds, allowing our hearts to guide us toward a life filled with joy, peace, and fulfillment.

With deepest gratitude for embarking on this journey together,

Your Gentle and Patient Guide

Madhu Sharma

Bibliography

Part One

Bilodeau, T. (2021). 'Managing intrusive thoughts'. Retrieved from: https://www.health.harward.edu/mind-and-mood/managing-intrusive-thoughts

Craig, J. (2020). 'Discovery of 'thought worms' opens a window to the mind'. Retrieved from: https://www.queensu.ca/gazette/stories/discovery-thought-worms-opens-window-mind

'How to Turn Your Negative Thinking Around.' Retrieved from: https://health.clevelandclinic.org/turn-around-negative-thinking

'20 Stoic Quotes on Managing Anger.' Retrieved from: https://www.orionphilosophy.com/stoic-blog/stoic-quotes-on-managing-anger

Pinchard, T. (2020). 'Negative Self Talk: The Tornado Effect - Train your brain to focus on the possibilities, not the limitations. Retrieved from: https://www.linkedin.com/pulse/negative-self-talk-tornado-effect-train-your-brain-focus-pinchard

Roy, S. (2022). 'R.A.I.N. Method of Mindfulness Meditation: A Precise Guide'. Retrieved from: https://happyproject.in/rain-meditation-technique/guide

Seif, M., & Winston, S. (2018). 'Unwanted Intrusive Thoughts.' Retrieved from: https://adaa.org/learn-from-us/from-the-experts/blog-posts/consumer/unwanted-intrusive-thoughts

Wang, Huang, Duke, & Yang (2017). 'Tai Chi, Yoga, and Qigong as Mind-Body Exercises.' Volume 2017. Retrieved from: https://www.hindawi.com/journals/ecam/2017/8763915

Part Two

Angel, G. (2017). 'A story about living in the present.' Retrieved from:

https://www.gregoryangell.com/2017/10/story-living-present-moment

Beach, S. R. (n.d.). 'Mindful studying: How to learn without losing your mind.' Retrieved from: https://leftbrainbuddha.com/mindful-studying-how-to-learn-without-losing-your-mind/

Greater Good Magazine. (n.d.). 'What is mindfulness?' Retrieved from: https://greatergood.berkeley.edu/topic/mindfulness/definition

Jayaram, V. (n.d.). 'Living in the present is true living.' Retrieved from: https://www.hinduwebsite.com/random/present.asp

Stenger, M. (2016, September 9). 'Interleaved practice: 4 ways to learn better by mixing it up.' Retrieved from: https://www.opencolleges.edu.au/informed/learning-strategies/interleaved-practice-4-ways-to-learn-better-by-mixing-it-up/

Taking Charge of Your Health & Wellbeing. (n.d.). 'What is mindfulness?' Retrieved from: https://www.takingcharge.csh.umn.edu/

Project Happiness. (2021). '8 mindfulness habits you can practice every day.' Retrieved from: https//projecthappiness.mykajabi.com/blog/8-Mindfulness-Habits-You-Can-Practice-Everyday

Part Three

Angela Duckworth, Journal of Personality and Social Psychology. Retrieved from: https://trickle.app/drip/21789-grit-is-a-key-factor-in-exceptional-achievement/

Cherry, K. (2023). 'Yin and Yang: How Ancient Ideas of Balance Can Help Your Mental Health.' Retrieved from: https://www.verywellmind.com/yin-and-yang-mental-health-7110781

Davit. (2018). Self-Care: '12 Ways to Take Better Care of Yourself'. Retrieved from: https://www.psychologytoday.com/us/blog/click-here-happiness/201812/self-care-12-ways-take-better-care-yourself

Furr N., Furr S. H. (2022). 'How to Overcome Your Fear of the Unknown.' Retrieved from: https://hbr.org/2022/07/how-to-overcome-your-fear-of-the-unknown

Gordon, S. (2020). 'Self-Compassion Makes Life More Manageable.' Retrieved from: https://www.verywellmind.com/how-to-develop-self-compassion-4158290

Marie. Bloomfield (2018). 'Fierce Self-Compassion: The Yin and the Yang of Self-Compassion: Mindful Path.' Retrieved from: Fierce Self-Compassion: The Yin and the Yang of Self-Compassion: Mindful Path by Natalie Sobel | Dec 29, 2020

Neff (2009). 'The Role of Self-Compassion in Development: A Healthier Way to Relate to Oneself.' Retrieved from: https://www.ncbi.nlm.nih.gov/pmc/articles/PMC2790748

Prabbhan, P. (2020). 'Spend Time with Yourself.' Retrieved from: https://www.deccanchronicle.com/sunday-chronicle/cover-story/020220/spend-time-with-yourself.html

'Stages of Sleep: REM and Non-REM Sleep' (n.d.). Retrieved from: https://www.webmd.com/sleep-disorders/sleep-101

Rogers, C. R. (1961). 'On becoming a person.' Boston, MA: Houghton Mifflin. Retrieved from: https://www.vdh.virginia.gov/workforce-wellness/wellness-topics/self-acceptance

Part Four

Shawber, A. (2019). 'Ten ways to be a Person of Substance.' Retrieved from: https://www.linkedin.com/pulse/ten-ways-person-substance-andrew-shawbe

Part Five

Brenner, A. (2016) 8 'Traits the Most Toxic People in Your Life Share.' Retrieved from: https://www.psychologytoday.com/intl/blog/in-flux/201608/8-traits-the-most-toxic-people-in-your-life-share

Eco Watch (2014,) 'Reasons Why You Feel So Good in Nature'

Retrieved from: https://www.ecowatch.com/10-reasons-why-you-feel-so-good-in-nature-1881977943.html

Fisher, H. (2019) 'Essence of Happiness: Small Things Matter.' Retrieved from: https://www.essentiallyyoucounseling.com/small-things-often/

Furr, J., & Furr, J. (2022). 'The Upside of Uncertainty: A Guide to Finding Possibility in the Unknown' Harvard Business Review Press. Retrieved from: https://hbsp.harvard.edu/product/10547

Hibbert, C. (2013) 'Living a Life of Purpose & Meaning: The Key to True Happiness.' Retrieved from: https://www.drchristinahibbert.com

Kim, D. (2021) 'What's a Toxic Person and How to Deal with Them.' Retrieved from: https://psychcentral.com/blog/whats-a-toxic-person-how-do-you-deal-with-one

Lickerman, A. (2010) 'Overcoming Obsession' Retrieved from: Overcoming Obsession | Psychology To-day.com

Luintel, S. (2022) 'Guide To 4 Ds of Time Management – When and How to use' Retrieved from: https://timetracko.com/blog/4-ds-of-time-management

Moshagen, M. (2018) 'The dark core personality'Retrieved from: https://content.apa.org/record/2018-32574-001

Oosterwijk, S. (2017) 'Choosing the negative: A behavior-al demonstration of morbid curiosity, Retrieved from: https://www.ncbi.nlm.nih.gov/pmc/articles/PMC5500011/

Sho, T. (2021) 'Kintsugi: Japan's ancient art of embracing imperfection'Retrieved from: https://www.bbc.com/travel/article/20210107-kintsugi-japans-ancient-art-of-embracing-imperfection

Prabhu. (2021) 'Vedic Approach to Overcoming Stress, Anxiety & Sleeplessness 'Retrieved from: Vedic Approach to Overcoming Stress, Anxiety & Sleeplessness | Vedic Management Centre (ve-dic-management.com)

'Stress: Coping with Life's Stressors 'Retrieved from: https://my.clevelandclinic.org/health/articles/6392-stress-coping-with-lifes-stressor

'The Biophilia Hypothesis' Retrieved from: https://psychology.fandom.com/wiki/Biophilia_hypothesis

'Real-life inspirational stories that touched the heart', Retrieved from: https://motivationalspeaks.com/real-life-inspirational-stories-that-touched-heart/

Stephen Hawking, Various authors (no specific publication date). Retrieved from: https://www.space.com/15923-stephen-hawking.html

Part Six

Shrimad Bhagavad Gita Text

'VivekVani Bhagvad Gita Chapter 1-18', Retrieved from: https//vivekavani.com

About the Author

Madhu Sharma is an accomplished author and the architect behind the wonderful book called "Taming the Monkey Mind." In this captivating self-help book, Madhu Sharma shares her insights and expertise on conquering the challenges presented by our busy and wandering minds. Through her engaging writing style and practical advice, she guides readers on a transformative journey towards clarity, focus, and inner peace. With Madhu Sharma's guidance, readers can learn valuable techniques and strategies to tame their restless minds and cultivate a more balanced and fulfilling life.

This remarkable individual is a retired director and founder principal of not just one, but two esteemed schools: Rukmani Birla Modern High School in Jaipur, and Vardhman International School, also in Jaipur. Additionally, she has served as the principal of Apex International School in Jaipur. With such extensive experience in the field of education, the author possesses a deep understanding of human psychology and personal growth.

"Taming the Monkey Mind" is the culmination of Madhu Sharma's life's work. In this enlightening self-help book, she distils her wisdom, offering practical strategies to quiet the mental chatter that often disrupts inner peace. Drawing from her deep well of knowledge in psychology, education, and counselling, she provides readers with a roadmap to overcome stress, anxiety, and self-doubt.

Made in the USA
Columbia, SC
21 February 2024

e4788caf-3bc0-4d53-b0d6-f7716c48d399R01